BEGINNING
IN
JERUSALEM

edited by

RUEBEN P. JOB

BEGINNING
IN
JERUSALEM

Tidings—Nashville

Library of Congress Catalog Card Number: 75-10373

EV032B

CONTENTS

Introduction

There is an old proverb which says, "The leaves want to rest, but the wind keeps blowing." There is ample evidence everywhere that the church wants to rest, to take her ease, to dwell in tranquility. There is also a growing awareness that the winds of the Spirit keep blowing and the church cannot be at rest in this age or in any other.

Many large conferences give their attention to study. Others give their attention to inspiration. And still others draw persons from the far corners of the earth for fellowship and communion. However, one of the participants in the Jerusalem Consultation was correct when he said, "This entire consultation is geared to action."

Throughout the addresses you will hear the challenge to go, and you will feel the urgency of the mandate given by our Lord to all Christians to make disciples.

This volume is a compilation of the addresses presented at the World Methodist Council Consultation on Evangelism held in Jerusalem in late November 1974. The consultation marks the first faint hint of the dawn of a new day of global evangelism. That is, there is a new sense in which the church is understanding itself and God's mission to the world. Emilio Castro says, "Mission does not go from us to them, but comes from God to all of us. God enlightens all of us to participate equally in his missionary movement: 'As the Father sent me, so send I you.'"

Thus, Jerusalem marks a new beginning for global evangelism. No portion of the world can now see itself exempt from the command to "go and make disciples." Further, no portion of the world can see itself paternalistically sending out the message to others. Rather, there is the growing awareness that every Christian is an evangelist and carries the responsibility of proclaiming and demonstrating the good news of God. In like manner, every portion of the world is the harvest field to which God sends his messengers of good news.

As you read this volume you will discover that each of the addresses points toward action. There is not a feverish endeavor to save an aging institution, but a faithful activity in obedience to him who said, "Go therefore and make disciples of all nations, baptizing them in the name of the Father and of the Son and the Holy Spirit, teaching them to observe all that I have commanded you; and lo, I am always with you, to the close of the age" (Matt. 28:19–20).

RUEBEN P. JOB

God's Call for Mission

Almost two thousand years ago at Bethlehem God launched the world mission of Jesus. In daring to proclaim 1975 as a year of mission, world Methodism is merely sharing in the initiative taken by God himself when he gave his Son to be the Savior of the world.

God was the first evangelist. Long before the birth of Jesus God sought to lead a rebellious humanity back into his purposes. In the coming of Jesus that purpose reached its fullest expression, mankind learning once and for all how much God loved the world.

Since the crucifixion and the resurrection of Jesus his living spirit has directed his mission, constantly probing into the human situation, seeking men and women who would be responsible to his will. When that response has been withheld his cause has tarried; when it has been given the world has seen some new expression of his love and power.

World Mission '75 represents an act of obedience by a world community of Christians called Methodists, and all who will join with them, to God's call to mission today. God has spoken and the church has answered. It recognizes that the world mission of Jesus is an unfinished mission. It is a confession of the deep need of humanity now. It is an attempt in penitence and trust to say, where he may lead we will follow. Hence at Bethlehem and Jerusalem, where it all began, we dedicate ourselves afresh to God's purposes in history.

As we set out together we must be sure of the mandate for mission. We must know the foundation on which the task rests. We must be able to declare our reasons for a new world thrust in evangelism, for trying to point to Jesus Christ as Lord and Savior for all people.

1. The Overflowing Love of God

The call to world mission comes directly from the heart of God. God cannot contain the goodwill which floods in his being for the creatures he has made. An overflow of divine love is the beginning of mission.

The whole world today needs to discover and rediscover the wonder, the glory of the love of God. Something has gone seriously wrong about our understanding of God. With cold and impersonal phrases such as *first-cause, ground of all being,* and *death of God* we have robbed God of warmth and meaning. We have turned God into a problem to be solved rather than a being to be known and enjoyed. We desperately need to hear the One who knew most about God saying to us: "When you pray say: 'Our Father who is in heaven.' "

Look at the facts which show that God cannot help himself. His nature predisposes him to endless self-giving. God continues to express his nature in the created universe. From the beginning of time his spirit has pointed forward, always leading toward a more developed and complete life. Nature has moved on from dead matter to living plants and trees, from motionless growth to living moving beings, from lower animals at last to men and women.

The Bible is the story of the redeemer God. From the first hour of man's rebellion God's nature responded not in judgment only but in love. To Noah and Abraham, he was a savior God. Through Moses he delivered the slaves in Egypt and in the great prophets of the sixth century before Christ he sought to redeem Israel from her sins.

Here in Jerusalem it is surely easy for us to celebrate

2

the mightiest of all God's mighty acts, the coming of Jesus. Around us are the reminders of the birth, the life, the death, the resurrection of him who is called the Savior of the world.

Yet the overflowing love of God was not exhausted at Bethlehem or Calvary. Soon Pentecost happened. The promise was kept: "I will pour out my spirit on all flesh." Through history that spirit has flowed on. When God found a Francis of Assisi, a Martin Luther, a John Wesley, new acts of redemption appeared. When mighty movements like the Reformation, the nineteenth century missionary movement, the ecumenical movement of the twentieth century occurred we knew God was still in action in his world.

The redemptive purpose of God in history has not ceased. Many of us in these despondent years should be ashamed of our faithlessness and despair. God has not turned his back on us. The overflowing love of God streams on, surrounding each of our lives, pouring its blessing into every area of life.

Faith and prayer, on our side, make possible God's fuller self-giving. Faithlessness, doubt, asking little of God, seem to dam up this power. Believing prayer opens the floodgate and the life-giving spirit of God pours through. Worldwide prayer is a prerequisite of world mission.

The love of God is the motive for mission. Why does a Christian care? It is a response to God for all he has done for us. Religion is grace and witness, service and gratitude.

Therefore we go on mission with joy. We shout the faith of the Bible: "O give thanks to the Lord our God whose steadfast love endures forever." We echo the authentic voice of early Methodism: "Love divine all loves excelling, joy of heaven to earth come down," and "O for a thousand tongues to sing my great Redeemer's praise." Because of what God is doing we invite people in every land to sing with us an old gospel hymn:

Out of my bondage, sorrow and night, Jesus, I come,

3

Jesus, I come;

Into Thy freedom, gladness, and light, Jesus, I come to Thee;

Out of my sickness into Thy health, Out of my want and into Thy wealth,

Out of my sin and into Thyself, Jesus, I come to Thee.

> William T. Sleeper
> "Jesus, I Come"
> [Baptist Hymnal]

2. The Predicament of Mankind

God's call for mission rises out of the need and predicament of the modern world. An hour of deepening crisis has tolled for humanity, and God as always is responding to it by a new declaration of his grace.

As we assemble here in Jerusalem we might well ask why Jesus came in what we now call the first year of the Christian era. Why did God not act a thousand years before, or a thousand years later for that matter? I believe God poured out his love in his Son Jesus Christ because of the need of humanity.

In that first century the predicament of mankind had reached crisis proportions. Moral sexual corruption had eaten far into Roman and Greek societies. The suffering of slave communities, the inhumanity of man to man, public sadism filled the earth. Religion was formal and dead among the Jews, while the rest of the world lived in the twilight of the gods, the deities of the day having lost all authority and power. God, hearing the plea of the people, as earlier the cry of the slaves in Egypt reached his compassionate heart, plunged into the misery and sin of humanity.

In calling us to World Mission '75 God is responding to the need of our time. I believe the world today is plunged into a deeper crisis, and the human family is in greater jeopardy, than we realize. This is an hour for

4

God, and God is acting in love.

The name of today's crisis is moral permissiveness. The everlasting right is in eclipse, lost in the murkiness of moral relativity. Ernest Hemingway aptly defined what is called the new morality: "Good is what you feel good after, evil is what you feel bad after." Hence anything, everything, becomes permissible. The moral chaos described by the Bible has come: "Each man does what is right in his own eyes."

Sexual corruption is far advanced in Western society. Millions are turned inward, wallowing in the lusts of the body. Fornification, adultery, and all the aberrations of true sexuality are seriously presented as valid, feasible, alternative lifestyles. Karl Menninger aptly asks: "Whatever became of sin?" Sexual sin has become a joke. The loveliness of purity is being lost in the surge of undisciplined desire.

Sex standards and civilization rise and fall together. When sensualism is in the ascendancy society is in peril. The delicate restraints between men and women go down. The basic unit, the family, begins to disintegrate. A pathetic form of addiction multiplies—sexual addiction. The human body becomes an idol, replacing God.

The names of today's crises are poverty, hunger, and starvation. Food and energy shortages, unemployment, uncontrollable inflation could be portents of a coming world famine. With ever more millions of mouths to feed, the exhaustion of the earth becomes a very present peril.

Who can comprehend or describe the suffering of the poor? To walk through a *favella* in South America, a black ghetto in the United States, an Arab refugee camp, a famine area of Ethiopia is to grasp a little of poverty's degradation. But to experience it, as a parent hearing a child cry for food and having none, to feel personally the pangs of hunger and to live with the hopelessness of it all—this is beyond us.

The poverty crisis for the Christian is reflected in the parable Jesus told of Dives and Lazarus. The rich man did not see the poor man at his gate. Nor do we. The affluent West consumes most of the food and the supplies of the earth. The United States, for example, with 6 percent of the world's people consumes 40 percent of its goods. Australia is so wealthy that the poorest of its citizens are rich by the standards of any land in the Third World. For the West the crisis is judgment—the judgment of God which falls on those who allow affluence to choke the wells of neighborly concern and compassion.

The name of today's crisis is the rejection of God. It is the irreligion which deprives personal lives and society of the flowing grace of God. The judgment of John Keble applies to our world: "The beginning and end of all of our troubles is that we have forgotten God."

The twentieth century reveals a new phenomenon: a widespread, deliberate repudiation of the fact of God. For the sophisticated society of England, America, and Australia, God does not exist. Throughout the Communist world God is officially banished. It is indeed "an age of atheism," to use Paul Schilling's phrase.

The consequences arising from God's absence are becoming apparent. The morality gap is widening. Socrates defined that gap: "Men know what is good, but do what is bad." A godless universe means a loveless universe, hence many live with a sense of loneliness, harshness, alienation. A pervasive mood of the meaninglessness of life has replaced an earlier general consciousness of guilt. There is appearing, especially among youth, a disillusionment with materialism and a craving to experience the transcendent, a spiritual hunger which will not be denied.

I tremble for the Western and the Communist world. The corruptions which flow from irreligion are far advanced. Cutting himself off from God, man is on his own. The judgments of God are beginning to work themselves out. Isaiah's warning begins to be relevant: "This iniquity shall be to you like a break in a high wall, bulging out and ready to collapse, whose crash comes suddenly at an instant."

The name of the crisis is that millions of people have

6

never heard of Jesus Christ. Because of the population explosion there are more people today being deprived of any conscious encounter with Christ than ever in history.

God's purpose, according to the New Testament, is that his Son should be known among all people. So rapid and vast has been the increase in the human family that the church faces its greatest challenge since the first century. In almost every land the task has moved beyond the resources of the church community. Yet, for the Christian, there is no escaping the summons of Jesus: "As the Father has sent me, so send I you."

Who can question that before so towering an hour of need God is speaking? To Christians everywhere his summons sounds loud and clear. World Mission '75 is one response to that cry. It is the answer of faith to the need and predicament of today's world.

3. The Inevitability of the Gospel

God's call for mission rests on the inevitability of the Christian gospel. There is literally nothing else save the Christian faith which can match the range and reach of the predicament facing the modern world.

World Mission '75 proclaims the biblical truth that Jesus Christ is irreplaceable, inevitable, and ultimate. There is no other name but Jesus who reveals the wonder and the fullness of the nature of God. There is no other universal Savior and Lord whose truth is valid for the First, the Second, and the Third World. There is no other whose liberating power reaches to the depths of human experience answering every demand which can rise from the sinful, suffering, sorrowing heart of humanity.

Jesus as God's revealer is inevitable. I wish to speak with sensitivity, for we meet here in Jerusalem sacred to the three great world religions of Judaism, Islam, and Christianity. God is known through many prophets and teachers, through many revelations of truth, but there is for the Christian no escaping the words of Jesus as

7

found in the Gospel of John: "No man comes to the Father but by me." Only through the revelation of Jesus do we find the Christian God, the God whom we experience as our heavenly Father.

Because of the God he reveals, Jesus comes to a humanity filled with frustration and helplessness offering salvation by faith alone. Albert Outler expresses the significance of this truth: "Self-righteousness is replaced by the righteousness of Christ. By faith and faith alone—uptight lives are relaxed, trapped lives liberated, arrogant lives humbled, soiled lives cleansed, slouching lives raised up to tiptoe, empty lives filled, life unto death turned into life unto life."

There is no "do-it-yourself kit" of salvation. Therefore the choice Paul discovered is stark: It is a losing moral struggle for trust in Christ. To a defeated humanity comes the thrilling news: "By grace are you saved, through faith, and that not of yourself, it is a gift of God."

The Jesus lifestyle is inevitable. The world today is experimenting with every conceivable alternative way of life. As a result moral confusion reigns. Light is being called darkness, and darkness light. Yet the truth remains, life and human relationships will work only one way, the Jesus way.

Radical holiness is the need of the world. How can sensual seaminess be cleansed save by people who live purely, making sex beautiful? How can gross selfishness be condemned save by the appearance of people who do live beyond self-interest, sacrificing openly personal gain for the sake of others? How will the loss of human dignity and worth be reversed save by people who reveal an innate respect and tenderness toward others? How will the cult of violence and war itself be challenged save by many becoming committed to nonviolence, to rejecting under all circumstances maiming and killing?

In John Wesley's vision of personal holiness the Methodist church has a revelant message for today. An earlier simple piety rejected alcohol and respected Sunday as the Lord's Day and sought sexual purity not only in action but, like Jesus, pushed it back into thought and imagination.

Now a larger piety must be added, one which will move in the area of world concerns. The mark of a Methodist, of a Christian, now must surely be seen in unremitting condemnation of racism in all its ugly and widespread forms. That mark is concern for millions of human beings who live with crippling poverty and unnerving hunger. It is bound up with a rejection of war and a deliberate choosing of the means of nonviolence in seeking social change.

The kingdom of God, God's reign in human society, is inevitable. The future lies not with the kingdoms of socialism or capitalism or communism, but with the kingdom of God.

A new world civilization must emerge or humanity will stagger on into chaos and darkness. We have come to the end of an era. Aggressive capitalism, oppressive communism, and competing nationalism will now only betray the people and exhaust the earth.

The towering issue is world poverty, and beyond poverty, survival. Almost unnoticed millions already are quietly starving, quietly dying. They are the first signs that world society is moving beyond the ability of the planetary support system to meet the demands made upon it. Famine will not remain silent. Ahead lies human misery beyond comprehension and as a result uprising, bloodshed, worldwide political upheaval, unless answers are found.

There can be no new world civilization without a massive attack on the terrible wastefulness of armaments. This hungry world spends $200 billion a year on armaments, representing 6.5 percent of the gross national product of the world. The annual expenditure means that the world spends three times more on armaments than on health, twice as much as on education, and armaments claim thirty times more than all the economic aid granted by the developed to the underdeveloped countries.

The colossal wastefulness of the millions of people

engaged in nonproductive military preparations is beyond calculation. Loose the 50 million people caught up in the military machine for productive work and the human scene will be transformed.

There will be no survival for millions without sacrifice by the affluent Western world. The dream of lifting others toward an ever rising Western standard of living is without reality. The result would be an impoverished world. The West must consume less if the rest of the world is to live.

We are very conscious that we meet today in Jerusalem amid the suffering and division of the war-torn Middle East. In the name of the Prince of Peace we plead with Israel and her Arab neighbors to search for ways of peace. There is nothing but disaster ahead unless retaliation gives place to reconciliation; unless "an eye for an eye and a tooth for a tooth" is replaced by the ideal of Jesus, "love your enemies."

Only fundamental changes of attitude by Israel and the Arab countries can bring peace: the acceptance of the fact of Israel by the Arab; the granting of justice to the Arab refugees by Israel; the re-drawing of boundaries on the basis not of war but of justice must occur. We plead that new initiatives for peace may be taken now, not after the tragedy of further warfare.

Austerity, the voluntary acceptance of a lower standard of living, a vast redistribution of resources, has become necessary. Urgently the appeal must go out for the rich to become poor in order that the poor may live, not in a heaven beyond time, but here and now.

World Mission '75 calls on all people to acknowledge God as supreme in personal and world life. Without repentance for the rejection of God the world will stagger into deepening chaos and disaster. People everywhere have listened to each other for long enough; it is time to listen to God. Only the authority and power of God can match this hour of humanity's need.

The enthronement of God would transform the world. God gives dignity and worth to every life. God places the poor on the conscience of mankind, requiring

10

that love of neighbor shall be above love of self. God quickens honor and justice, keeping people decent when no one is looking. God is the last defense against tyranny in human society. God preserves the earth, saving it from destruction. God releases creative forces into society, ever making all things new. God makes peace, giving hope amid the perils of a nuclear age. God alone gives meaning to living and purpose to history.

So here in Jerusalem we shout the cry of John Wesley which awakened England from the sleep of death in the eighteenth century:

> "Awake, sleeper
> Rise from the dead
> And Christ will shine upon you."

4. The Call to the Church

God's call for mission is directed squarely to his church. This call is God's declaration of faith in the church which the risen Christ has established.

World Mission '75 affirms its faith in the church. It rejects the strange heresy which would accept Jesus Christ and have nothing to do with his body, the church. The time is overdue for Christians to speak up for the church. The church is complacent, but it is not corrupt. The church is old, but it is not without new life. The church is imperfect, but it always was open to sinners. The church is strong, but resources are dedicated to service for the people. The church is weak, but it has defied the power of the state. The church fails, but let it never be forgotten that for two thousand years it has shielded and communicated a divine gospel.

The call to mission is a very personal call. On a hill not far away the commission to witness was first heard: "You shall be my witnesses in Jerusalem, Judea, Samaria and to the ends of the earth." It is a summons to a person-to-person evangelism.

Every Christian is an evangelist. This is the dream and the strategy of mission. It is lay men and women who

11

live in the world. In the fields, by the counter, at the bench, in the home, at school, at play, the witness must be given. There is no escape from the personal call to witness. Still the challenge comes: "Let the redeemed of the Lord say so."

Authentic Christian living must stand behind every act of witness. Without it there is no credibility, no power. Archbishop Soderblom of Sweden described what happens when words and actions flow together: "A saint is one who rebels against God's might. Saints are such as who show clearly and plainly in their lives and deeds that God lives."

The Christian community makes the love of God visible. If ever Marshall McCluhan's statement is true, it is of the church: "The medium is the message."

What a strategy Jesus devised. His plan was to place all over the world small communities of people gathered around his risen presence, sustained by worship and the sacraments, sharing fellowship together, witnessing and serving in the world. From these small centers of spiritual power he believed the story of Jesus would encircle the globe and penetrate the needs and heart of the people.

World Mission '75 is true to the mind of Jesus. It represents no global master plan, directed from some world center of power. It is simply a call to every local neighborhood church to be about its central business of proclaiming the gospel and making disciples in the name of Jesus.

The local church has so much the world craves. Amid the loneliness and alienation of mass society, the church offers a warm and intimate fellowship. In a world which often does not hear the cry of the frail and the helpless, it can be the voice of the voiceless. In the cramped materialism of many lives it can mediate the unseen and the transcendent, satisfying the deepest yearning of the human heart.

From Jerusalem therefore the call goes forth. Every local church is invited, in an unbroken chain, to go on mission. Each center, thinking, praising, planning, experimenting, following its own leading of the Spirit is asked to witness. By openness to the Holy Spirit and boldness in faith, by struggle and courage, the mission will live. It will be in the furnace of effort that another, whose form is like the Son of God, will join us all.

The church is a global fellowship. This is a new fact of the twentieth century. What an achievement the Christian church has registered in the last two hundred years in becoming a universal company. International Christianity is a reality.

World Mission '75 is mobilizing Christians all over the world for mission. It represents a new missionary vision, a new missionary strategy. Here are no sending and receiving areas, no paternalism or spiritual superiority. It is Christians everywhere going witnessing together, helping each other in the one task of offering Jesus Christ to the whole world.

I thrill to the vision. As we share in mission in the heart of Sydney in Australia we will be joining in a company of Methodists and other Christians no one can number. I see that village church in Fiji and Tonga with its matted palm roof. I see that solid concrete church in Leipsig bravely witnessing under communism that Jesus is Lord. I see the Aymara Indians gathering on the altiplano in Bolivia. I see a crowded cathedral-like church in the United States, its people the very salt of American society. I see the plane of the flying padre coming down on the private airstrip of a lonely homestead in the Australian outback. I see the vital churches of Asia, of Malaysia or South Korea, where young people predominate, singing of the love of Jesus. I see the historic churches of England where Methodism began, struggling but faithful.

A Christian is a man or a woman to whom Christ has entrusted his world. World need requires a world mission. Daunted by the sin, the hardness, the complexity of the world, uplifted by the gospel, we humbly yet confidently go on mission together. We shall dare together to say to all mankind: "Look, the Lamb of God who is to remove the sin of the world."

13

chapter two

T. WALLACE KOOMSON

The Challenge of the Gospel for a New World

I find three concepts in the challenge of the gospel for a new world that are being brought together more and more in our day. Each of the key terms of the topic—challenge, gospel, and new world—contains within itself a whole world of argument and story. A new world! How new? Geographers referred to the Americas as a new world in terms of discovery, after Europe had been known for centuries. But that is not what we mean. By *new* we understand a qualitative improvement in the world. Even here there is another problem: People's understanding of a better quality of life differs—for some it is more money, bigger cars, more leisure; for others it is a spiritual quality. I mean a world in which man realizes himself fully as one created in the image and likeness of God.

Next the gospel, which means good news. But what good news? Of God's action in Jesus Christ to reconcile rebellious man to himself. But what does that mean? If you look around, you see diverse and discordant answers given by the churches, the very institutions which are proclaiming the good news. So how can the world take the church and her gospel seriously? Why add another chaos to the already chaotic world?

In my part of the world, we are beginning to see what has been the experience of the West for a long time: the

15

increasing complexity of life and the aimlessness that goes with it. Many African Christian leaders are becoming increasingly vocal on the question of the gospel within the context of our traditional life and thought and the impinging forces of industrialization and technology. This desire to hear the gospel in a new way has led increasingly to the use of the expression *African theology*. Inherent in this search—whether for African theology or for authenticity or relevance—is the recognition that times have changed. However, the gospel is unchanged and unchanging, and the question is whether it can speak to the world of today. Perhaps the adjective *new* is not quite appropriate; the human failings of greed and cruelty, and the like, are not and will not be new. And yet, our world can be described as new in the sense that we have greater opportunity than before to remove the ills that plague it. The advances that have been made in the field of learning are immense, although these advances have not brought us the dignity and freedom and peace which mankind has long sought.

People of the new world are asking: Why should something which happened in the first century after Christ be of relevance to us in the twentieth century with a higher level of development than that of the first century? Is it not a crazy claim? Surely, there have been many deaths, but why do we say that the death of Jesus is relevant to us in a unique way? Furthermore, some of the claims of the gospel are apparently too fantastic.

Why should we take a social revolutionary who appears to have laid claims to divinity seriously? Is he not a crank who makes divine claims? Is it not the scandal of particularity to lay claim to one man, Jesus Christ of Nazareth, as the turning point of history? And when that gospel was proclaimed in the first century after Christ was it not "a stumbling block to Jews and folly to Gentiles" (1 Cor. 1:23, RSV)?

Perhaps the gospel is not what we need in our world. What if we Christians are wrong in believing the gospel of Christ? What if the basis for the truth of the gospel of

16

Christ is false? Suppose we come to the conclusion that the gospel of Christ is not superior to other teaching and ideologies that are being offered today for man's salvation. What then?

We have raised several questions, doubts, and misgivings about the word *gospel*. Is the gospel to be ruled out of court in the twentieth century on the grounds of being out of date, irrelevant, invalid, and untrue? In short, how can the gospel fit into the "brave new world" of our time and of the future? And that is the third challenge.

It is easy to raise questions. Answers are difficult to come by or proffer. Fortunately, I have been saved the task of offering answers to these problems because the topic, "The Challenge of the Gospel for a New World," assumes that the gospel has, in fact, a contribution to make. And my task really is to outline what sort of contribution it can make.

Nevertheless, I cannot let it go without one comment. The fact of history is that many—high and low, rich and poor, the intellectually gifted and intellectually poor, old and young, men and women from all the countries that make up the globe—have for nearly two thousand years embraced the Christian faith. Were they all deluded, misled? Was their judgment impaired, were their critical faculties doped by the personality of Jesus and his gospel? No! It is difficult to believe that it is all a mistake. They have built a religious tradition for us.

We are asking for tradition to be taken seriously, this especially in an age when there is compulsive rebellion against tradition and what is old. Yes, I recognize that tradition can be a dead weight; it can easily become a security instead of a challenge. But I am arguing that any genuine advance has to be rooted in the past. As Dean Inge, that great English churchman and author, once said, "Originality is generally the power to see old things in a new light." All real progress is made when there is a combination of the old and new, an acceptance of the historical continuity of thought and ways with such modifications of them that they are

17

born in a new light and in a new day.

The twentieth century has seen the unprecedented development of civilization with scientific invention as its chief weapon and catalyst. Man has been able to split the atom; he has conquered space. Faster communication, the revolution of our time, making it possible to fly from Accra to Jerusalem in one day or to know instantaneously in Accra what happens in New York, is eloquent testimony to man's achievement as a "creator."

Emboldened by the indisputable achievements of science, it is argued by some that science is the key to the new world. Our trouble, we are told, is that hitherto scientists have had no real hand in the ordering of human life. Given the authority, the test tube and the crucible will do all that is necessary for the birth of a brave new world. That line of thinking is eloquently advanced by Philip Radagise, the forty-year-old head of a university biocybernetics laboratory, in Aleksandr Solzhenitsyn's *Candle in the Wind.** He said: "We live for science, we breathe science, but if in the process the money just gushes out, it's a pleasant sensation, believe me! But surely I don't have to try to prove to *you* that science is the light, the meaning, and the interest of life for people such as ourselves? To run through the second half of the twentieth century with the relay baton which Newton, Maxwell, and Einstein have held and then at the finish line to hand it on to the twenty-first century?" The message is quite clear: Science is the key to the new world.

And yet our own inventions have become a plague to us. I am impressed by the reaction of Alex Coriel, the forty-year-old mathematician in the same book. He said to Philip Radagise: "Philip! I have the feeling that we will not need to hand on the relay baton." At that point Philip comes in: "Nuclear war you mean?" It means that our own inventions are now threatening to destroy us. Chemical research which has produced anesthetics and antiseptics has also produced mustard gas. The same mechanical processes which have given us automobiles, radio, television, has also made possible the fearful devastation of total war. Alex Coriel again says: "Science has successfully proved that it's very good at serving the cause of tyranny." The same Alex Coriel, reflecting on his several years as a teacher of mathematics and physics, has this to say: "At first I was quite content. But then . . . I began to understand that my teaching was partly a lie. I was stuffing them with theorems, draftsmanship, talk about Space. But I wasn't preparing them to be able to resist the heartlessness and calculation they would meet with in life."

Yes, it is "partly a lie" when it is said that science alone is the key to the new world, because knowledge is amoral. There is a certain soullessness about science. Our human intellect to its last fraction, as well as our spiritual forces, are being employed in the service of producing material goods. But is that all? Do we take cognizance of the spiritual force behind all our efforts? More frightening is the thought that this worship of science is, in a way, the worship of our intellects. Alex Coriel again puts it well for me: " 'Oh, great science!' That's the same as saying, 'Oh, we great minds!' or even more precisely, 'Oh, great me!' People have worshiped fire, the moon, and the wooden idols—but I'm afraid that worshiping an idol is not so pitiful as worshiping oneself."

This is where the trouble lies. With the worship of science goes a certain defect in human nature, some radical evil in man himself, which makes things in his new world go wrong, which turns the works of his hands to his own destruction.

Others peddle the idea that the key to the new world is human progress without God. "The evil of the world, such people think, is only a state of man's development. A few more years and man will grow out of it. Slavery came and is gone. Humanity has long left behind barbarism and savagery." Some believe in the perfectibility of human nature without any reference to God.

But is this really true? There is no evidence whatever

that we are better than our forebears. A world which has seen two world wars with enormous carnage and the ineradicable results of delinquency still is faced by environmental pollution, racism, exploitation of the poor by the rich, the suppression of the so-called inferior race by the so-called superior race, superior knowledge, superior color, superior language. Our scientific developments have been, in part, responsible for the development of more efficient weapons of destruction. When then can we seriously maintain that the perfectibility of man, without God, is the key to the new world? Has our increasing conquest of nature seen a corresponding conquest of ourselves—our greed and lust, our will-to-power, our fears? While we are gathering knowledge and power with ever-increasing and measureless speed, our virtues and wisdom, our moral and spiritual values have not shown any notable improvement as the years have rolled by. In starvation as in terror, in warlike passion as in cold intellectual frenzy, man today as before performs the most terrible and wicked deeds to his fellowmen.

Others will proclaim political planning as the essential ingredient for an ordered and happy new world: "Federation abroad and common ownership at home" are the clichés. A United Nations organization or an Organization of African Unity with an international police force will guarantee world peace for a new world. The removal of tariff and frontier barriers, together with an equitable distribution of commodities, will ensure plenty in a new world. The abolition of capitalism will create a new brotherhood of unselfish, disinterested service. Terms like *self-reliance* and *Operation Feed Yourself* are in vogue in my country, Ghana.

Of course, there is some truth in all these. They are desirable. But to see them as the sole key to the new world is naive. The lesson from history is as yet not contradicted, that such political idealisms tend to be another attempt of man to build his tower of Babel. When and where on the globe and throughout the successions of civilizations has man succeeded in

20

building a just and righteous society? Man will fail to realize a just society as long as his political blueprints for utopia are content to leave out the pride and egotism so characteristic of man, the darling self-will of the human heart.

Another approach is education and social development. Man, they say, goes wrong because he knows no better. He must simply be taught to do right. And he must be placed in more congenial surroundings. After all, who could be respectable in a slum?

One does not underestimate the influence of education and environment in constructing a new world. But my question is, Can you change a man's perverse nature simply by sending him to a university to be equipped for a new world? Does education eradicate a man's greed and lust and self-assertion? It is astounding to go through history to find some of the best brains put to perverse use. It is a *non sequitur* that when a person knows what is right, he will do it. Ovid and Paul put it well: "I see the good, I approve of it but I follow the evil." It is all very well to say "Knowledge is power." Yes, it is power. But power to do what? To blow civilization to bits? To crush the weak? To drive away owners of lands from their rightful places? To exploit the rich resources of the underdeveloped world to the greater benefit of the so-called developed world?

Nor is it true that environment alone is responsible for the evils of the world. If we were to go through the catalogue of sins in Galatians 5 in any international gathering, there would be no doubt that no one group had a monopoly on evil or on any of the sins. Selfishness and greed, barbarity and lust are as rampant in the developed world as in the underdeveloped world. Marxism is totally mistaken in seeking the root of human evil only in the social environment.

It is facile to think as some have done that man has only to turn a new leaf and make a fresh start. Man is beset at every turn by his selfishness, his greed, his pride which tends to turn his achievement into an instrument of his doom. Man needs a massive external

21

aid to save him from himself. It is at this point that the Gospel offers a timely rescue to a falling world.

The gospel proclaims that God in Jesus Christ can do for man what man can never do for himself; that God alone can heal humanity's sickness and restore a disintegrating world. It doesn't repudiate man's own efforts to build a better world, but it points to our futility if God is left out of the picture. Political planning, education, sociology, and science all have their place—and a very important place—in the new world, but the gospel is something quite distinct from them all. It is good news, not good advice—the good news that in a carpenter of Nazareth God has visited and redeemed his people; that the power of Christ, and it alone, can subjugate human self-will and become the driving force in a new and better world. In the church, with the spirit coming to a burning focus in worship, the new life given by God is made available to all who will receive it.

Father Martin d'Arcy in his *No Absent God* quotes Gabriel Marcel to stress man's need of a power outside himself in order to attain his true manhood:

> There is a side to the universe which is not turned towards us: we are limited, and yet there is a reality which is inexhaustible. We are not our own masterpieces. What is deepest in me is not of me.

In further support of this, he quotes the following from Boris Pasternaks's *Dr. Zhivago:*

> Now what is history? It is the centuries of systematic exploration of the riddle of death, with a view to overcoming death. That is why people discover mathematical infiinity and electromagnetic waves, that is why they write symphonies. *You can't make* such discoveries without spiritual equipment. And the basic elements of this equipment are in the Gospels. The Gospel is the clue and the power to save man from himself.

The Secular Implications of the Gospel

The gospel demands personal decision and commitment. It is essentially a way of life, and the Christian has to live his faith in the world among his fellowmen in his society. Indeed the scriptures know nothing of a solitary religion. It is in his everyday living, in his everyday decisions, in his attitude towards his fellowmen, in his hopes and fears that the Christian can live his faith and contribute towards the building of the kingdom of God in his day and age.

But the secular implications of the gospel do not only affect the individual Christian, but also the church as a body. "The church is her true self only when she exists for humanity." Far more important than our central halls and magnificent churches is the need for the presence of the church in the forefront of the war to eradicate poverty, hunger, ignorance, disease, discrimination, and prejudice. It must stir the social conscience of the nation as John Wesley did in eighteenth century England.

Perhaps I can illustrate the secular mission of the church in this new age by referring to the situation in West Africa where the church has immense opportunities to get involved in the task of nation-building. In Ghana, for example, where barely 18 percent of the children of secondary school age can get to secondary schools, and still fewer gain admission to universities, there is a pressing need to build polytechnic and vocational institutes which will enable as many young people as possible to equip themselves technically and professionally with skills to cope with life in a fast developing country.

In the field of agriculture, the churches could join the Operation Feed Yourself campaign by establishing church farms all over the country. Such effort will also help to stress the fact that farming could be a respectable and rewarding occupation in Ghana.

From a world perspective, the growing gap between the richer and the poorer countries should be a matter

23

of great concern to the Christian who takes seriously the challenge of the gospel and its secular implications.

It is not enough for churches in the developed countries to send donations to their less fortunate brethren elsewhere. Much as these donations are appreciated, the essential need is to offer them something of that type of aid that will assist them to stand on their feet. I mean the lending or the export of skilled men, capital and technical know-how to cooperate with other factors of production in these new countries to generate such economic activity as will help to raise the living standards of these lands.

The current debate is whether the world can feed itself. In Africa, there are virgin lands which combined with capital, management and technical know-how from the developed countries will make an impact on the world food situation and the economies of these young countries.

There are wonderful opportunities for fruitful cooperation between the churches in the developed and the underdeveloped countries to raise the living standards of the latter.

What I have said about the secular implications of the gospel is summed up by Edward Everett Hale in his poem "The Nameless Saints":

What was his name? I do not know his name.
I only know he heard God's voice and came,
    Brought all he had across the sea
    To live and work for God and me;
. . . .

And I?
Is there some desert or some pathless sea
Where Thou, good God of angels, will send
    me?
Some oak for me to rend; some sod,
    Some rock for me to break
    Some handful of His corn to take
        And scatter far afield,
        Till it, in turn, shall yield
            Its hundredfold of grains of gold
    To feed the waiting children of my God?
Show me the desert, Father, or the sea.
Is it Thine enterprise? Great God, send me.

24

The challenge of the gospel in this new age will be feeble, lacking a sense of direction, unless our preaching and living the gospel is deeply rooted in a life of prayer, in the practice of the presence of God. "They that wait upon the Lord shall renew their strength" (Isa. 40:31). "Be still and know that I am God" (Psalm 46:10).

The gospel is an invitation and a challenge to man to set his heart on the higher talents, to seek the still higher path in his daily life, within the context of the secular world. It is the assurance that the God who revealed himself in the face of Jesus Christ is ever ready to lift man above his narrow human limitations and offer him the glorious liberty of the children of God, making him a co-partner in the task of finishing the new creation.

Perhaps the mood of this hour is summed up in the familiar but profound words of the *Prayer Book* in 1928: "Go forth into the world in peace. Be of good courage; hold fast that which is good. Render to no man evil for evil. Strengthen the fainthearted, support the weak, help the afflicted. Honour all men, love and serve the Lord, rejoicing in the power of the Holy Spirit."

That is the challenge of the gospel for this new world and for all times.

---

*Quotations on pp. 18-19 are from Alexsandr Solzhenitsyn, *Candle in the Wind* (Minneapolis: University of Minnesota Press, 1960), pp. 45, 49, 50, and 102.

The World Challenges the Church

"All that you want us for is pew-fodder and to get the money out of our pockets." The words were flung at me by a shop steward on the floor of a British factory. Under different circumstances I should have wanted to argue that we did want to see people in the pews or wherever the meeting place of the church happened to be. There are things, such as worship, fellowship, teaching, and training for which Christians need to be together. I would defend, too, the church's need for money. The church is a voluntary organization and if it is to exist in any organized form it must rely on the gifts of its people.

But this, of course, is not all for which we want to interest people. Indeed we should hotly insist that church attendance and money are far from being our primary concerns. Our motives are on an altogether higher plane. That may be so, but to the many who are not numbered among us it does not always appear to be the case. It may surprise us, and we may feel deeply hurt to realize it, but the shop steward who reacted so vigorously to the presence of a parson in his domain was speaking for thousands who see us as concerned first and foremost with being able to say that we have a good congregation and that we are paying our way.

The world challenges us to make evident the sincerity of our motive. The world has learned from bitter experience to be suspicious of those who come to it in the guise of saviors. Some countries have seen the Communist come, supplying arms, building dams, and providing food. Other lands have been the target of the capitalist entrepreneur who has established industries, opened up the mineral resources of the earth, and built houses for the indigenous and indigent people.

The advent of Communist and capitalist alike has created employment that has resulted in improved standards of living, better houses, and well-fed babies. All this may be seen as commendable, and indeed it is. But disillusionment comes if it emerges that the underlying motive of the whole exercise was not the real benefit of the people, but was designed to obtain power, exert influence, exercise control, or to amass personal wealth.

The world can be forgiven if it looks with some questioning at the motive of the church, for we have not always succeeded in avoiding paternalistic attitudes, a spirit of superiority, or an air of condescension.

Our motive must not only be clear to us, but must be clearly seen by others. That motive is to give expression to the love of God for every man, woman, and child in the world, and to interpret that love in terms of what it means to live in God's world. The pauper must be absolutely sure that we are as concerned for him as we are for the prince, and the prince must know that he is seen equally with the pauper as a child of God. We are not concerned with princes and paupers as such, with rich or poor, black or white, young or old, men or women, good or bad—we are concerned for people, all people, every person.

The world challenges us to make that concern real in down-to-earth terms by our readiness to be identified with God's people in the world. That means, in the first place, simply being where the people are. One of the wonderful things about Jesus was that he lived out his life among the people. He was where they were; he was accessible to them, angry if anyone would have prevented anybody from being near him. He taught in their synagogues, walked in their streets, stood with them in their marketplaces, was interested in their work and play, ate in their homes, watched by their sick ones. He "came with the helpless and hopeless to dwell"—not a fleeting visitor with a clipboard and sheet of questions conducting a sociological survey with which he would return to his comfortable air-conditioned office and the giant computer—he came to dwell with the people, fully identified with them.

Sydney Carter's modern song asks the question "When I needed a neighbor, were you there?" It goes on to identify what it means to be a neighbor: "I was hungry and thirsty, were you there? . . . I was cold, I was naked, were you there? . . . when I needed a shelter. . . , when I needed a healer . . . ,when they put me in prison, were you there?" And the answer: "Wherever you travel, I'll be there!"* That is the answer that begins to put flesh on the bones of our professed love of mankind, but it needs to be expanded.

The world challenges the church to recognize that love for all people involves a commitment to the belief that every human being has the right to live on this earth in freedom, unmolested and undisturbed by anyone. It is not enough to bring temporary relief to people in their need, leaving them in their bondages, with the assurance of "pie in the sky when they die." Today, the right to live a truly human existence is denied to millions of people. Half the world is underfed and undernourished—not much freedom there, beyond the freedom to die. Millions live under oppression and persecution—no freedom there. In my own country, part of the so-called affluent West, tens of thousands of people still live in slums or grossly overcrowded conditions.

All these people are on the conscience of the church. The work of a host of relief agencies, many of them serviced by Christian people, is beyond praise, but that work is not enough. We cannot sleep easily in our beds—those of us who have beds in which to sleep—until all people are able to live that truly human existence of which the Denver Call to Mission and Evangelism speaks.

But if the world challenges us to realism, let it too be realistic. The church is a minority in almost every land and a small minority in most. Alone the church cannot hope to achieve the goal of human freedom. Let the world face its own challenge—let it bring pressure to bear on the rulers and governments of the nations to take seriously the need to secure for every individual his/her basic rights.

The world challenges us not only to strive to secure, but also to respect the rights of every individual. When Christianity is true to its Lord, that is what it does. Jesus believed in the sacredness of human personality and consistently refused to violate it. He would not force men, not even force them for their own good, to follow him. He looked out over this city and wept over it. "How often," he said, "have I longed to gather your children, as a hen gathers her brood under her wings, but you would not let me." Although he foresaw the consequences of that rejection, he would not force them.

Philip Potter, general secretary of the World Council of Churches, in a recent address to the Synod of Roman Catholic Bishops, said that our witness was corrupted when cajolery, bribery, undue pressure, or intimidation was used.

The world rightly challenges the church to respect human personality—but let the world heed its own advice. The church cannot but be anxious as it sees how some, in their zeal to secure rights for the deprived, in the process violate the rights of those who have already inherited them. The commentary on a new filmstrip issued in Great Britain by the Methodist Missionary Society and the United Society for the Propagation of the Gospel to launch their joint study course on Latin America begins with the words "Any time that human lives are violated in their integrity, that is violence."

While any such violence exists, the church can only be distressed.

Thus far we have been thinking about the individual, but the Christian gospel is concerned with more than the rights of individuals. It is deeply conscious of the corporate life of society and the individual's responsibility in that society. I will defend to the last the right of every man to live his own life undisturbed and unmolested without domination or threat from anyone. At the same time I would argue equally strongly that every person has a responsibility to the society in which he/she lives and indeed to the world of which he/she is a part. I would go further and insist that that responsibility may, and almost certainly will require of the individual a voluntary surrender of some part of his/her rights.

The world challenges the church to accept that responsibility, and it is here that the church faces one of its greatest tests today. Our motive may be clear—it is love for all mankind. As an expression of that love we may become involved in the community, identifying ourselves with the people, living among them in all their hopes and fears, joys and sorrows, successes and failures, seeking for them their fundamental rights as human beings. But the question is: How much are we prepared to sacrifice for the sake of mankind?

In 1835 the first British missionaries went to the Gold Coast in West Africa. At Cape Coast, where they landed, there now stands the splendid Wesley Church. On the front of the pulpit in that church there is a tablet bearing this inscription:

> Sacred to the memory of our earliest missionaries, the Rev. Joseph R. Dunwell, the Rev. and Mrs. George O. Wrigley, the Rev. and Mrs. Peter Harrop, 1835–1837, whose remains lie buried under this pulpit.

It was one of the most moving moments in my life when in 1969, as the British representative to the Ghana

31

Conference, I had the privilege of preaching from that pulpit. As I stood there, looking out over a great sea of faces, the faces of the Christian men and women and children of Cape Coast, my thoughts went back to those three men and two women who went out to what was known then as the white man's grave. They went out and must have known in their hearts that they would never go back. Within two years every one of them had died.

Few of us, perhaps, will be called upon to sacrifice our lives, but what are we prepared to sacrifice? Are we ready to be inconvenienced, to be put out, for it to cost us something to show and practice God's love for all people? I long to see more signs today of a readiness, in the words of Charles Wesley:

> To spend and to be spent for them
> who have not yet my Savior known;
> fully on these my mission prove
> and only breathe, to breathe thy love.

When the church responds to that challenge it will indeed be credible in the eyes of the world and it will then have the right to challenge the world—you make your sacrifices, you leave your security, you surrender your rights, you give yourselves to Christ, accept him as Lord and Savior, follow him wherever he leads you, and let your lives be a living of the love of God for all people.

Salvation Today—An Evangelistic Approach

In January 1973 a world conference on Salvation Today took place in Bangkok under the auspices of the Commission on World Mission and Evangelism of The World Council of Churches. I quote from its official report:

> In the power of the Spirit Christ is sent from God, the Father, into this divided world "to preach the Gospel to the poor, to heal the brokenhearted, to preach deliverance to the captives and recovering of sight to the blind, to set at liberty the oppressed and to proclaim the year of God's favour" (Luke 4:18). Through Christ, men and women are liberated and empowered with all their energies and possibilities to participate in his Messianic work. Through his death on the Cross and his resurrection from the dead, hope of salvation becomes realistic and reality hopeful. He liberates from the prison of guilt. He takes the inevitability out of history. In him the kingdom of God and of free people is at hand. Faith in Christ releases in man creative freedom for the salvation of the world. He who separates himself from the mission of God separates himself from salvation.

The salvation which Christ brought and in which we participate, offers a comprehensive wholeness in this divided life. We understand salvation as newness of life—the unfolding of true humanity in the fulness of God (Col. 2:9). It is salvation of the soul and the body, of the individual and society, mankind and "the groaning creation" (Rom. 8:19). As evil works both in personal life and in exploitative social structures which humiliate humankind, so God's justice manifests itself both in the justification of the sinner and in social and political justice. As guilt is both individual and corporate, so God's liberating power changes both persons and structures. We have to overcome the dichotomies in our thinking between soul and body, person and society, humankind and creation. Therefore, we see the struggles for economic justice, political freedom and cultural renewal as elements in the total liberation of the world through the mission of God. This liberation is finally fulfilled when "death is swallowed up in victory" (1 Cor. 15:55). This comprehensive notion of salvation demands of the whole of the people of God a matching comprehensive approach to their participation in salvation.

At the recent World Congress on Evangelism held in Lausanne, a group of delegates produced a document called "A Response to Lausanne." This was not a contradiction of the Lausanne Covenant but, rather, a deepening of its theological content and basic affirmations. This document says:

The *evangel* is God's good news in Jesus Christ; it is good news of the reign he proclaimed and embodies; of God's mission of love to restore the world to wholeness through the cross of Christ and Him alone; of His victory over the demonic powers of destruction and death; of His Lordship over the entire universe; it is good news of a new creation, a

34

new humanity, a new birth through Him by His life-giving Spirit; of the gifts of the messianic reign contained in Jesus and mediated through Him by His Spirit; of the charismatic community empowered to embody his reign of shalom here and now before the whole creation and make his good news seen and known. It is good news of liberation, of restoration, of wholeness and of salvation that is personal, social, global and cosmic. Jesus is Lord! Alleluia! Let the earth hear His voice!

The communication of the evangel in its fullness to every person is a mandate of the Lord Jesus to his community. There is no biblical dichotomy between the word spoken and the word made visible in the lives of God's people. Men and women will look as they listen, and what they see must be at one with what they hear. The Christian community must chatter, discuss, and proclaim the gospel. It must express the gospel in its life as the new society, in its sacrificial service to others as a genuine expression of God's love, and its prophetic exposing and opposing all demonic forces that deny the Lordship of Christ and keep people from being less than fully human. God's people must pursue real justice for all humanity; they must act as caring trustees of God's creation and its resources.

There are times when our communication may be by attitude or action only, and times when the spoken word will stand alone. But we must repudiate as demonic the attempt to drive a wedge between the word spoken and the word made visible.

The mission of the church must be seen in relation to this saving purpose of God which incorporates the fullness of the human race, the fulness of the whole of creation. The church is a people aware of the divine purposes, who sees them in action, who accompanies and proclaims them.

God's mission thus seeks to overcome the total alienation of man—the alienation of man from God, from his neighbor, from himself, from nature—to overcome all opposition, to bring everything to an ultimate harmony in which his love is recognized as sovereign. Churches and individual Christians are therefore taking part in a battle of the Spirit in which God himself is involved; local mission and transcultural mission are different ways of collaborating with God in the overall process of liberation. In other words, we live in an era of world mission. We cannot and must not distinguish between the service which we give to God and our neighbor in our immediate vicinity, and service given in a remote corner of the planet. The important thing is that the immediate and the distant should be integral parts of a conscious and intelligent participation in the spiritual battle, in which we join with God to struggle towards the goal of the redemption of all things in Jesus Christ.

In this holistic interpretation of the mission of God we can see the important role of the individual prayers of the believer, inasmuch as his struggle for the health of a child, his fight to bring meaning and direction to the life of a teenager, the longing to save a home, participation in the struggle for justice for workers, the political struggle of a nation, the search for more just structures at the continental level—all these are part of a continuing process in which God's spirit is seeking to make his love a signpost for all the paths of life.

Thus the dichotomy between the spiritual and the material disappears. Proclamation and service, liturgy and social action, the call to repentence and changes in social structures, are not independent of each other; they are not contradictory realities. Rather, they are different forms of participating in the great mission to which God calls us. It is the task of the Christian church to tell the world who it is who struggles, what is the goal of the struggle, and, in the perspective of the cross, to participate by accepting suffering and sacrifice where necessary to overcome human alienation and to challenge the whole community to make the changes which can lead to the hope that God promises. This understanding of mission allows us to free ourselves of paternalism. Mission does not go from *us* to *them*, but comes from God for all of us. God invites all of us equally to participate in his missionary movement: "As the Father sent me, so I send you."

To evangelize is to invite persons to recognize the kingdom which is coming in Jesus Christ, incarnate in a king who stands beside the suffering in order to work with them to re-establish a relationship with God, with their neighbors, themselves, and the whole cosmos. The resurrection of Jesus Christ confirms this in the ultimate destruction of the forces of evil, in the validity of the pardon which is granted, in the hope of a new day and a new man, a new humanity, a new cosmos with Christ. The gospel of the kingdom is to be proclaimed to every individual, and also to the powers and principalities. Man, in the fullness of his humanness, in the midst of a society which belongs to history and to the universe, is the one who receives the call of the message of the cross and who is thus invited to join in God's redeeming and saving mission. Evangelization, then, is not an escapist message of religiosity, but rather demands participation in the struggle to transform all the alienating factors of human life.

This participation is inspired by the cross and affirmed in the resurrection. It finds its style in the cross, its hope in the resurrection. But there are some questions to be asked about this affirmation. History has shown that the preaching of the cross of Jesus Christ has given rise time and again to a self-centered concern for one's personal salvation, one's own pardon, one's own experience, one's own future. It is limited to redemption at the level of the individual, taken out of the context of his social and historical relationships. We must recognize that it is possible for persons to convert even the sacred into the banal. However, the biblical revelation offers an invitation to follow Jesus Christ, to submit ourselves to the discipline of the cross by surrendering our lives. At the same time, this security of salvation has sometimes been considered as the affirmation of a non-theological and objective fact that belongs to a past history and without existential relationships.

The Christian affirmation that we die with Christ in order to be resurrected with him to a new life could be interpreted as the mechanical transmission of an objective reality from the past to our present life, but it can and must also be interpreted as participation with Christ in God's mission. The pardon of the cross and the new life in the resurrection are true inasmuch as we take our place in God's liberating struggle.

A further possibility of distorting the message of the cross would be to consider it as offering only the pardon of individual sins, isolating us further from the social groups to which we belong. Many white Christians are faced with the agonizing question of how they can be forgiven for being white. How can we free ourselves from the collective guilt which falls upon our nation, our ethnic or social groups? We all belong to social groups whose guilt we share to some extent. The pasts of our nations live on in us. But the cross of Christ speaks to us of the pardon granted by God not only to each person but to the whole of human history, so that we can take up the task of transforming it, using the present realities as possibilities. The cross frees us from a neurotic obsession with our past sins to turn our present situation into a challenging field of action in which God expects our militant participation. The word of the cross is the word of grace.

Recently another objection has been raised to the evangelistic message of the cross—that it tends to be a form of Western or Christian exclusivism which appoints itself as sole bearer of salvation, adopting an attitude of superiority over other religions and ideologies. There is always a danger of arrogance, or claiming to possess the truth. The gospel is not an invitation to recognize our wisdom, but rather an invitation to witness to a gift which we have received unexpectedly, through grace, to make a contribution to the human dialogue and to serve our neighbor, to join him in the search for common goals. The message of the cross eliminates all possibility of arrogance. God himself did not choose to enter into human history by impressing mankind with his power, but by participating in man's need—in the manger, in taking the way of sinners, and finally dying on the cross. Evangelistic preaching ceases to be exclusivist and becomes credible when it demands nothing for itself but guides men and women to him whose style of life is reflected in his wounded hands and side.

But we must ask a more radical question. At a time when the nations of the Third World are seeking independence from colonialism and imperialism there is a danger that evangelistic preaching which demands that we fix our attention on the person of Jesus Christ will, in effect, act as an element of division which diverts energy from the urgent priorities of our peoples. At a moment when mankind is seeking reconciliation with nature, a Christian demand which insists on man's historical dominion over nature runs the risk of becoming merely a further obstacle to the solution of our problems. Some ask whether it would not be much more responsible and perhaps more Christian if we renounced our Christian identity for a while to join in silence with those who are trying to face the problems and limitations of mankind creatively and sacrificially. This is a serious question. And yet, the existence of a Christian church working to share its faith and convictions with the rest of the world can have tremendous importance in the struggle for liberation, the search for our own identity, the development of a national culture, and reconciliation with nature. The Christian faith as discipleship with Christ is a permanent invitation to militancy. Our traditional Christian formulae will do little to shake neo-pagan Europe or post-Christian North America from their present style of life. But we can challenge them on the basis of obedience and militant participation in man's vital struggles.

M. M. Thomas said at Bangkok:

It is precisely at this point that the victory of the Cross is relevant. The mission of the Church in this context is to be present within the creative liberation movements of our time which the

Gospel of Christ itself has helped to take shape, and so to participate in them as to be able to communicate the genuine gospel of liberation—from the vicious circle of sin and alienation, law and self-righteousness, frustration and death into the new realm of Christ's new humanity where there is forgiveness and reconciliation, grace and justification, renewal and eternal life. It is this message that will liberate the liberation movements from the false spiritual structures of meaning based on idolatrous worship of schemes of self-redemption, and thus redeem their creative impulses from self-destructive tendencies, enabling them to achieve their inner rationale of human emancipation. Our message of Christ's salvation is ever the same; it is the call to men and nations to turn "from idols to serve a living God" who 'has translated us from the domain of darkness into the kingdom of his dear Son' Jesus Christ. In him we have divine forgiveness and are delivered from the ultimate spiritual insecurities of the self that seeks justification through its own efforts, and are "made free to love." Today "idols" and "darkness" have a new character; and "love" too must have new implications. (*IRM*, April 1973, Vol. LXII, No. 246, pp. 164–165)

chapter five
ELISA R. OCERA

Women in Mission

I was asked to talk on "The Role of Women in Mission." There is a slight but significant change in the topic. I have deleted the word *role* because it carries a meaning which, for me, is negative as it is associated with a traditional and cultural distinction between the sexes, relegating woman to specific tasks and positions in the church and society because her sex is inferior and subordinate to the male. A more lengthy treatise on this point will be taken up later in my address. The topic as modified is "Women in Mission."

I would like to begin with two basic assumptions, and these two are expressed in the key words of the topic, namely, *mission* and *women.* First, in this assembly we understand, accept, believe, and are committed to this mission of which we speak, which is God's own mission. One theologian has said that it is God's action as revealed in the life, teachings, ministry, death, and resurrection of our Savior Jesus Christ. Here we affirm and commit ourselves to the total gospel which is for all humanity. As we look at the gospel, which is Christ himself, we see him in his power renewing the inner life of the individual through forgiveness, love, and compassion. Christ ministers to persons by making them whole and opening the possibilities of their personhood,

41

and by helping them to realize and fulfill themselves as full total human beings, responsive and responsible. The Bible calls this conversion; some call it renewal. But whatever term we may call it, we affirm that it is Christ's power that transforms our individual lives, which tend to be egocentric and selfish, into lives that can be spent in concern for others. But to stop there at a personal relationship with Christ is to be unfaithful to the whole gospel. At the beginning of his ministry Jesus made clear his mission: "The Spirit of the Lord is upon me, because he has anointed me to preach good news to the poor. He has sent me to proclaim release to the captives, and recovering of sight to the blind, to set at liberty those who are oppressed, to proclaim the acceptable year of the Lord" (Luke 4:18–19, RSV). Here we see that Christ's ministry is not only personal; it is also corporate. When Christ makes a person whole he not only reconciles the person to himself but also to his social and natural order. In the same manner, when Christ lays claim to a community, he reconciles persons within it: persons to God and persons to persons. This means then that if the church is to be faithful to the mission of her Lord, the church must continue to nurture the growth of individuals as free persons in Christ, to develop Christian personhood, and to help individuals to attain a continuing sense of spiritual renewal through worship, study, reflection and meditation, fellowship, and prayer. But the nurturing is not an end in itself; this is but the equipping of the believers to achieve their common task in the world, to be agents of justice and a strong voice against injustice and exploitation, and to work with others for the development of the world and society. In the past and even in the present, the church has been guilty of stopping with the first aspect of the gospel; the church has been guilty of bypassing the wounded, of not standing up for the voice of the poor, the oppressed, and the dispossessed, of tolerating social, economic, and political injustices. We feel that the Conference on World Cooperation for Development of The World

42

Council of Churches held in Beirut in April 1968 was in the correct direction when it declared: "We Christians admit our share in responsibility for the world's divisions and hatred." Therefore, as the church takes up the mission of Christ, she confirms that his spirit is a power that renews the world, individuals, groups, societies, the whole creation. In the language of *Populorum Progressio* (encyclical, Pope Paul VI, 1967) of The Roman Catholic Church: "the Church fosters human progress in the nations to which she brings the faith; that the aspirations of men to transform this world and develop are shared by her; . . . and for that reason that in so doing she is true to her Founder." Gyula Nagy, the Hungarian theologian, puts it in succinct and vivid language which I am borrowing to sum up what we have tried to say regarding the mission to which we in the church have been called: "God acts in two ways: in the *outward* world, through structures and law, and in the *inner* being of man through faith. But both actions of His love have one goal: the whole man and the whole world."

Second, we in this assembly accept and believe that there is no distinction between men and women insofar as their personhood is concerned. When we refer to women in mission we refer to them as an integral part of the body of Christ, used of God and by God, without any distinction to their sex. We refer to the openness of their hearts, the responsiveness of their beings, and the commitment of their lives to his mission and to the object of his mission, which is the whole world. Of course, the fact that a woman is still speaking on "Women in Misssion" witnesses to the fact that the assumption has not been translated completely into action and reality. The reality is that the church cannot yet, at this point, say to the world and mean it: "There is neither Jew nor Greek, there is neither slave nor free, there is neither male nor female; for you are all one in Christ Jesus" (Gal. 3:28, RSV). It is precisely because man has desired to measure his fellow beings and the world to his stature that he distorts the image and

43

meaning of his being. It is from this that Christ liberates us, and it is also in those institutions which man has built to perpetuate his designs that Christ's renewing power is needed.

To perpetuate the traditional and cultural belief that women are inferior to men and that a woman has status only in relation to her husband or her children is to say really that the point of reference of woman's being is man—which makes man a God unto himself in relation to woman! This is definitely contrary to the Christian faith. We affirm that God is alone the ground of our being—he is our point of reference with regard to our beginning, our life on earth, and to the life hereafter. If the church is faithful to the mission of Christ which is the liberation of persons from cultural and social structures that make people humiliated and enslaved, abandoned and deprived, then the church must be at the vanguard for the changing of basic attitudes and beliefs towards women. Otherwise, women will always be regarded as inferior beings like ethnic and cultural groups, and they will always be relegated to stereotyped roles and positions which the church and society have determined for them as "fit for women."

A very concrete example of the sad state of the shortage of women in levels of decision making in the church (one of those "unfit" for women) is underscored by the Study Commission of the 1972 General Conference of The United Methodist Church. The commission discovered that the shortage is more acute in the local church situation. The group found women in these organizations and activities which have been rather traditionally ascribed to them: education (63 percent), missions (70 percent), worship (37 percent), and the council on ministries (49 percent). At the same time the group noted the predominance of men in boards like the administrative board, committee on finance, board of trustees, pastor-parish relations committee—all crucial in determining policy and direction for the local congregation.

Can we imagine how much power and force could be mustered if the full potential of both men and women of the church could be harnessed toward the fulfillment of Christ's mission? Women would not then be encumbered by the frustrations, the handicaps, the difficulties, and the pressures which they still have to face and work against in order that they be accepted as full persons—not as men—by the church and society.

Women of the church, however, in spite of the existing situation, or in some cases because of it (thus, they have to come together as women) are *organized* for mission—they are in mission. The accent is on *organized.* Let me cite a few examples.

A good case of highly organized church women is the United Methodist Women of The United Methodist Church in the United States, which is the successor to the Woman's Societies and the Wesleyan Service Guilds. The purpose of the organization which counts on 54 percent of the total membership of The United Methodist Church clearly reflects their direction, their projects, programs, and involvements: Christian personhood, supportive fellowship, social involvement, global concerns—quite an order! But Theresa Hoover, associate general secretary of the Women's Division, believes that many committed lives organized for mission can do the task: "Our potential as United Methodist Women organized for mission on behalf of the kingdom of God through The United Methodist Church is unlimited! We know what we have been and who we are. We also know that we must go forward still on behalf of the kingdom through The United Methodist Church. We must keep alive our spirit of mission, our contacts with other women's groups in this land and others, we must seek allies with those who share our concerns and commitments."

That was in 1972. Two years later, the Women's Division made a report published in *Response* (April 1974) on the financial commitment of United Methodist women and the crucial role their financial support plays in the total mission program of the church. For this year the Women's Division anticipates an income of

$13,893,656 with by far the largest portion (98.9 cents for every dollar) coming from the undesignated gifts of United Methodist Women. The report ends with this statement: "The undesignated gifts of United Methodist Women, particularly the pledge to missions, provide the single largest source of income for the Board of Global Ministries, and for world and national mission programs."

Another example is the World Federation of Methodist Women which is an affiliate of The World Methodist Council. With its motto "To know Christ and make him known," the Federation seeks to aid in establishing Christ's kingdom among all peoples and in all areas of life; to share the abundant life of Christ through evangelism, healing ministries, education, and social services; to assist in the promotion of the missionary spirit throughout the world parish; to seek, with women of all lands, fellowship and mutual help in the building of a Christian world order. The program and projects of its around ten mission members in nine regional areas, with sixty-one units cover: evangelism, medical work, education, literature, children, youth, home and family life, rural projects, economic justice, international friendship, temperance, and world peace.

Then there is the Church Women United which sponsors, among other projects, the World Day of Prayer, managed by an International Committee which is made up of fifty-three women representing thirty nations. This is a worldwide grassroots example of ecumenical Christianity. In the early part of this year, it sent out Causeway '74 teams of women to different parts of Asia to study the needs and problems of the countries and to seek ways of helping promote justice and peace.

In Asia, women have banded together across national and international lines to form the Asian Church Women's Conference, integrally related to the Christian Conference of Asia (formerly the EACC). The fellowship promotes loving concern for each other through prayer and helping one another. It supports its projects through the Fellowship of the Least Coin to which every woman contributes monthly the least coin of her country. It has raised more than half a million dollars for projects in different parts of the world in helping the poor and the needy. In its Fifth Assembly held in Bangkok in October 1974, the women from Asia spoke of using the Asian Church Women's Conference as a channel of reconciliation; pressed for education for all women in Asia which is the key to making women realize their selfhood and their potentials as persons; encouraged women to seek positions of responsibility in all areas where they can influence the processes of decision making; urged the church to be more aware, to work more and continuously at its responsibility for the development of the whole person and all persons; and finally, to initiate joint action projects with people and groups of other faiths in matters of social concerns in local and national situations.

Lest we create the impression that nothing is happening at the grassroots level, listen to these terrific experiences of women lost in mission:

In Japan, the National Federation of Kyodan Women's Societies formed committees to study the education of school children. They were after the basic concepts in the textbooks, making sure that these did not idealize the past and lead their children to "imperialistic objectives." The women used the mass media—TV on a nationwide scale and the press—to air their findings and evaluation! The federation operates a retirement home for women pastors, pastor's widows, and other Christian workers on an annual budget of Y 1,800,000.

In California, women joined ranks with the farmworkers union and supported them during their strike. Commenting on the vital role which these women had in the union, the vice-president said: "We couldn't have a union without these women. Their sacrifices have been unbelievable. And the participation of women has helped keep the movement nonviolent."

In New Delhi, the Mobile Program is providing

much-needed care for the children of mothers who have to work. In this case, care is provided for the children of migrant labor families whose particular skills make them in great demand in the large cities of India, like Delhi.

In the Philippines, the National Women's Society of Christian Service sent the first missionary to Okinawa, which actually started the overseas mission program of The United Methodist Church. Up to the present, the women take care of 60 percent of the support of the church's world mission program. Moreover, the Board of Women's Work administers funds for scholarships, loans to students, retirement pensions for women workers, exchange visits of women leaders, kindergarten work, literature and work budgets for the different commissions on women's work.

This can go on and on. The breakthroughs for women in many parts of the world have been significant although there is much left to be desired. However, you and I are keenly aware of and know that the frontiers of mission are expanding and widening and that those frontiers encounter the ugly faces of famine, drought and other natural calamities, poverty, oppression and exploitation, the escalation of militarism in developing countries, the galloping population and its associated problems, industrialism and ecological imbalance, inflation, and many other problems. These enormous and staggering problems need all the brain, brawn, powers, and skills of all committed Christians to work with others for the salvation of mankind and the whole world. God in Christ continues to call you and me to the task and mission at hand, not as men or women, but as persons who are willing to be co-workers for the liberation of the whole person and the whole world. Ultimately then it is not women in mission but Christians in mission.

New Evangelists
for an Old Evangel

Jerusalem the golden, with milk and honey blest;
Beneath thy contemplation sink heart and voice at rest.
I know not, O I know not, what joys await us there
What radiancy of glory, what light beyond compare.

Such was St. Bernard's vision of the *heavenly*
Jerusalem—based, of course, on his medieval image of
this *earthly* city where we are met. Here we are, eight
centuries later, having reversed the order of Acts 1:8,
having come *from* the uttermost parts of the earth *to*
Samaria and Judea and finally to Jerusalem itself. What
intentions have brought us here, what expectations,
what perceptions of the shattering paradoxes that every
sensitive visitor quickly discovered here? Mt. Zion, the
Holy Sepulcher, the Wailing Wall, the Haram
Esh-Shariff—all so close together and all vivid reminders
of deep chasms and bitter conflicts that have left painful
memories and alarming portents: the Star of David, the
Crescent and Star of Islam, the Crusaders' Crosses.
Together, they generate an aura of unhallowed holiness.
This, then, is the city that above all others, for me at
least, is the sign of God's ongoing agony in and for a
world that keeps on breaking his heart. "O Jerusalem,
Jerusalem, . . . how often would I have gathered thy

children together, as a hen doth gather her brood under her wings, and ye would not" (Luke 13:34, KJV)—and we are dull of heart indeed if we do not hear this word as addressed to *us, now.*

Here is where it all began—*our common history as Christians!* Here's where it went from: northward to Damascus and Antioch, eastward to Edessa and India, westward to Greece and Rome, and thence to those uttermost parts that most of us call home. This, of course, is the valid sequence of our evangelical witness: always first wherever we are and thence as far as our love and usefulness can stretch. For evangelism, in essence, is *the outreach of love:* the outreach of Christ's martyrs (witnesses) and Christ's servants—always in Christ's Name and Spirit. Christian witness always speaks of God's downreaching love and grace, and calls men and women to an upreaching faith and worship— into new levels of participation in that new humanity in Christ through the Spirit that the Incarnation has always been aimed at. Downreach, upreach, outreach—this is the great cosmic mystery of salvation. And we have come here this week to renew our sense of the reality of this mystery, and to rededicate ourselves to its expression in *our* several ministries of outreach and service—wherever and whatever they may be.

But our gathering here falls at a moment of unprecedented global crisis—crisis piled on top of crisis—in every part of the world (and yet more clearly visible here than almost anywhere else in the world). We have grown accustomed to speak, somewhat too glibly I think, of three different "worlds" on just one planet, but the fact is that none of them is doing very well and all are fearfully interdependent. No global community has been achieved and none is in sight. Who can deny, or ignore the increasing instabilities and demoralizations in every major nation in the world, or the worldwide energy crunch that threatens both developed and developing countries with synchronized disaster? Who is unaware of hunger and famine on a global scale, or that the dangers of nuclear holocaust are escalating year by year? The world as we have known it for the past four centuries is dissolving before our eyes and the human prospect—on human terms—is grim on almost any score you can name. C. P. Snow was recently asked (on American TV) what he regarded as the main difference between the world he grew up in and ours today. What struck me most in his answer was that it was instant and reflex: "the absence of a future!" For the first time since the idea took root in Western Europe two centuries ago, the vision of human progress has begun to fade—certainly in the minds of most of those who have begun to calculate the limits of human growth on this planet.

Moreover, the specifically moral predicament of humankind remains as baffling and tragic as ever, even though it is usually perceived nowadays in rather different terms than it was two centuries ago. Last year, a great American psychiatrist, Karl Menninger, published a thundering indictment of modern morality—or immorality—under the title *Whatever Became of Sin?* His unsurprising answer turned out to be that sin has had a name-change ("social dysfunction") plus a face-lifting (in our "permissive society") but that it is still flourishing mightily—in the economic and social injustices that oppress so many and in the tidal wave of antinomianism and social pathology engulfing "Western culture" and many other parts of the world as well. The vision of a fully human community on earth has become blurred (even for the utopians), human misery spreads, the news from all over is disheartening.

Now it may very well be that many of you would prefer to diagnose our situation in other terms. There may even be some of you whose prognosis of the human future is more cheerful than mine. Let that be. For, in any case, we would all agree, wouldn't we, that humankind's bad news is deep-reaching and daunting. And I would also hope that we agree that this *new* crisis is, in some sense, a refocusing of an ancient question and a specific answer to that question that gave the Christian movement its first beginnings—less than a mile from here, on that first Pentecost long ago. The question is: What is God's *good* news to man's *bad* news? Bad news-good news, sin-salvation, bondage-liberation, alienation-reconciliation, despair-joy, death-resurrection—pairings like this are abundant in the history of Christian proclamation. But how are *we* to formulate and live out *our* version of God's evangel in Christ—our gospel to those who, on the one hand, are prisoners of their own unbelief, and to those who, on the other hand, are victims of "man's inhumanity to man"?

Your answers to these questions constitute your theology of Christian evangelism. The incarnation of those answers in a credible lifestyle is the measure of your ministry as a Christian evangelist. These then are the burning questions before us in these days: (1) the clarity and validity of our *theories* of evangelism, and (2) the quality and fruitfulness of our evangelistic *practice*. The world, insofar as it will notice this meeting at all, will judge us by these two criteria, above all.

And yet even to define our task in these terms reminds us that the cause of evangelism is currently in dire confusion—and not least because of its recent surge into ecclesiastical high fashion. As I struggle to keep up with the rush of literature in this area, the story of the Tower of Babel keeps popping into my head, unbidden. Older evangelicals, naturally enough, keep on calling what they've always been doing "evangelism" (with some very interesting efforts to update it). And they are gaining strength in world Protestantism overall by comparison with the waning of the dominant liberalism of the past one hundred years. Moreover and increasingly, they are laying a new stress on the essential linkage between salvation and social justice. At the same time, however, most of the current coterie-theologies (liberation theology, political theology, female theology, futurism, etc.) have begun to profess *their* allegiance to the cause of evangelism, too, claiming the label for what *they* are doing. The current issue of the social action house organ of my own particular denomination [*engage*] is all about this new evangelism—with comments on "the two warring camps" ("conservatives" and "liberals") together with a prescription for peace between them. It also includes a typical thesis: that the authority of Holy Scripture should be understood as analogous to the authority of the Constitution of the United States (which is shockingly bad jurisprudence, to say nothing more). This, of course, is only a minor incident in a worldwide phenomenon of evangelism as a new Christian frontier. Very much more important was Bangkok (1973)—which identified evangelism with social and political change—and this has become The World Council of Churches' official line ever since (with, however, a vigorous dissent from the Orthodox). Lausanne, this past July, was a peak experience for most of its participants but its subsequent follow-up, as far as I can tell, has been on the meager side. The Fourth Synod of Roman Catholic Bishops has just concluded a month-long exercise in *apparent* futility in its efforts to formulate a general consensus on its chosen theme, "The Evangelization of the World." It was, however, a deeply significant *event*, in part *because* of its real struggle and real candor. Alongside these large organized events, there are myriad related phenomena (mostly spontaneous): old charismatics and new ones—new modes of spirituality which are giving some of our "official types," in the mainstream churches, real problems.

Now, is it possible for us here this week to gather up the best in all these ambivalences and to find a hopeful way forward? Can conservative evangelism become socially involved merely by weaving social action rhetoric into its pronouncements? Can social action Christianity become evangelistic merely by liturgical additives to its utopian rhetoric? For that matter, is evangelism all this much a matter of *rhetoric* and *ideology*, in the first place? Is it possible that we have become *infatuated* by our rhetorics and deluded by our naive faith in the power and effect of church—or conciliar—pronouncements? Do we really believe that when a group of Christian leaders approve a resolution (or a statement drafted by a still smaller group of partisans) that this is really a momentous *deed*—or, conversely, do we suppose that reticence is *prima facie* evidence of some dereliction or failure? The truth is that we have vastly overrated the impact of ecclesiastical statements on public policy and, therefore, have vastly underrated the force and effect of actual Christian martyrdom (witness to Christ in life and death) and actual service (in life and death) on the part of those millions of local groups where the Gospel truly lives or dies. Indeed, if pronouncements and lobbying could save the world, the deed would already have been done, twice over, by my own church alone!

This, then, will be one of our temptations this week (as always): to depend on rhetoric overmuch (and I who say this am a rhetorician by trade). Our *main* job in these days, as I see it, is to explore and discover what consensus we may have, or can achieve, in *actual* answers to three perennial but newly urgent questions about evangelism—and to examine our actual commitment to such *actions* as might translate our best insights into *deeds with real consequences:*

1. What is God's evangel in Christ—the good news that we may proclaim and live out?

2. Who are they who are to be evangelized?

3. Who are they who are properly ordained evangelists, authorized for the ministries of martyrdom and service?

There are hundreds of ways to speak of God's evangel, and none can exhaust its mystery, or exclude other formulations. But all of the valid ones center on Jesus Christ and his redemptive ministry. The earliest version would seem to have been Peter's declaration, on Pentecost, that God had made Jesus (crucified for *our* sins) both Lord and Christ. The Pauline and Johannine versions are even more terse: "Jesus is the Lord."

"Jesus *is* the Lord"—it sounds so simple but its implications are staggering. It means that an actual man, one of us (the *homoousion hemin* of the Definition of Chalcedon), once walked this very same land, died on "a green hill *not* so far away," and yet also is Lord and Savior of your life and mine, Lord over sin, bondage and death, Lord of the human past (with all its ambiguities), Lord of the human future (with all its forebodings). Jesus Christ is Lord and Savior—to the glory of God the Father—and he calls all God's children to the hearing of faith and the life of discipleship. God was in him reconciling the world to himself (which we've often twisted around as if it read 'God was in Christ reconciling *himself to the world*'!). In Jesus, God's cosmic secret was disclosed (viz., his willingness to pardon repentant sinners by his grace without any merit whatsoever on their part). In him, God's personal reality was fully and humanly revealed, God's kingdom of righteousness bodied forth in a landmark life.

But what does Christ's Lordship mean? That every knee should bow and every tongue confess it? Yes—but more: that God's righteous rule in human hearts should recreate a truly human community in this world, providing a truly hopeful human future for all God's people, in and under his gracious providence. It means repentance and conversion, which means radical change and a new openness to change. Never ask of personal and social holiness which is prior; *neither* is authentic without the *other.* The kingdom of God is *within* you (*entos humōn*); the kingdom of God is among you (*entos humōn*). The same kingdom is both deeply subjective *and* urgently social. The ambiguity of that preposition *entos* is itself a part of God's revelation!

God's evangel is a hope-stirring word from God *to* men and women *through* men and women: it speaks of human origins and ends, of God as our first and final sustenance, of our sin and demoralization, of God's reconciling love in Christ, of the Holy Spirit at work creating holy persons and a holy community. The gospel is a joyful word about God's trustworthiness and grace, and yet also of his moral imperative that we should love him above all else and our neighbors in and from our love of him. It is an invitation to fellowship in the body of Christ, where all members have their own distinctive gifts and tasks in God's design to raise up a fully human community, on *this* earth, in this life.

This, of course, is only one man's way of speaking to the mystery of salvation as he has glimpsed and experienced it. What is *your* version? Does it center in Jesus Christ? Is it deeply rooted in faith and love? Is it creating a Christian lifestyle defined by service, social action and undaunted hope? If it be so, let us join hands and hearts—and let our rhetorics subordinate themselves to our actual agenda as Christians.

But, *secondly*, who are they who are to be evangelized? This is a tricky question and many of its conventional answers seem to me to be wrong, in the light of what probings I've been able to make in Holy Scripture *and* the Christian tradition. The answer, "those who otherwise would be damned to hell," carries with it, by assumption, a doctrine of reprobation that is unscriptural and un-Wesleyan. Another answer, "the unchurched," ignores the tragic fact that the ripest missionary field in existence today is precisely the *church!* This, of course, is what got John Wesley into trouble and, from the other side, what prompted Richard Graves's complaint about the early Methodists: "They are trying to plant the Gospel in a Christian country!"[1] A third answer, "the heathen, the deluded followers of false gods," ignores Wesley's very interesting (and strangely ignored) notions about what he called "the salvability of the heathen" and it also fails to repent of Christianity's shameful record in many of its proselyting methods in missionary history (bribery, coercion, colonialism, etc.). It is certain that Wesley was not a universalist, but it is equally certain that he taught a doctrine of (1) universal redemption, of (2) the prevenience of God's grace, and of (3) the universal presence and initiatives of God's Holy Spirit—in *all* human hearts and religions. Faith in Christ does not imply the repudiation of all of God's other self-revelations, but rather their rectification and fulfillment. "Think not," said Jesus, "that I am come to *destroy* the law, or the prophets: I am not come to destroy, but to fulfill (Matt 5:17, KJV). And this must be a prime rule for us in our evangelism as well as in all sincere inter-religious dialogues.

For evangelism is *Christian love in outreach:* outreach to *all* God's children (whomsoever, wheresoever, whatsoever) to whom our witness and service might conceivably communicate God's love in Christ—and our own. Our part is less to proselyte than to follow up on the Spirit's prior initiatives—if, as, and whenever. We are ambassadors of Christ's own gracious hospitality ("Whosoever will . . .") and not executioners of St. Augustine's terrifying, "*compel* them to come in."

Then, thirdly, who are they who are properly ordained and authorized as evangelists of God's evangel in the world? The conventional answer ("the clergy," "evangelists," missionaries, bureaucrats, et al.) is profoundly misleading. I would never deny that all these people are and ought to be evangelists, but I'd want to emphasize that they share their evangelistic ministry with *all* baptized-confirmed-converted Christians—since evangelism is, first and last, a ministry of the Christian *laos!* Clerical ordination is to the representative, sacramental ministries of the word, sacrament and order in the church (*the church sacral*). Evangelism, on the other hand, is distinctively the ministry of the *laos*, which is *the church visible in the world.* Evangelism is, therefore, secular Christianity at its best. It is Christian martyrdom (witness) and service *in the saeculum* (in the Christian's daily round): at home, in the community, anywhere, everywhere. For it is God's people at large who are Christ's martyrs and servants; without them, the main job of martyrdom and service goes undone, except by clerical samplings. *We* may be deceived when we let the *cleros* substitute for the *laos* in "secularizing" the gospel, but *the world* is never deceived. They always look behind our clerical showcase and see what the reality is amongst the Christian *amateurs*—those whose witness to the Lord Jesus and whose service of his brethren spring from their sheer love of it all—out of their sense of joy and gratitude, vivid or dim.

Who was it that turned the world upside down in Christianity's early centuries? The apostles and their successors? Well, yes—in a way (in a *crucial* way). But nothing much would ever have come to their labors if it had not been for those obscure, nameless people who went about their martyring and their serving—crumbling barriers between Jew and Gentile, male and female, bonded and free, throwing new bridges over old chasms between races, classes and cultures. Those early Christians were less concerned to make history than to prepare for its climax—which, even yet, is still "on the verge." It was Judas who first politicized the Christian movement—and he botched the job, as others after him have done. It was unconverted Peter who came up with the first "orthodox" confession of Jesus' deity—and then went on to deny him, which goes to show that orthodoxy alone is never enough. Both these patterns (unconverted minds unprepared for the practical consequences of their good ideas) have been repeated so often since that one might conclude that Christians are slow learners! When, for example, Christians came to actual political power in the fourth century, they made a fearful mess of the business—and history has repeated this same dismal story ever since. Indeed, I cannot think of *any* so-called state-church or church-state society in which I'd be willing to live, given almost any other choice!

It is a sad irony that we have learned so little from John Wesley on this point. Clearly, for him, the Gospel call was to repentance, pardon, and new life in Christ. Its ethical mandate was always love (perfect love at that) to God and neighbor. Its social agenda was a new breed of humanity—liberated from the fear of man, bound by gratitude to God. His secret was that vital balance which he sought and found between "faith alone" *and* "holy living" (the *root* and the *fruit* of

Christian existence). One might say that, since Wesley, our Methodist conservatives have tilted his balance too much toward "faith alone," while our Methodist liberals have overreached on the "holy living" half (carefully changing its traditional labels—always on the verge of Pelagianism [or over it]). Neither seems to have understood Wesley's insistence on "faith alone" as the *threshold* of salvation, and on "holy living" as the *lifelong task* of hallowing all of life in all of its occasions. This combination really was revolutionary (as Bernard Semmel has recognized in an important book entitled *The Methodist Revolution* [1973]). For Wesley, *and his people*, knew that evangelism is not merely one item amongst many on the Christian agenda. It *is* the Christian agenda in *outreach toward others*, within the church and without. And always, its most effective agents are living Christians who witness to Christ and who serve their brethren and sisters in the course of their ordinary human enterprises.

One of Wesley's lesser known pieces is a brief satirical essay called *A Short Method of Converting All the Roman Catholics in Ireland* (1752). Its thesis is so unrealistic that it sounds almost cynical: Let the Protestant clergy and people in Ireland "only *live* like the Apostles, *preach* like the Apostles [and serve like the Apostles] and the thing is done."[2] He goes on to describe how the Apostles lived and preached and served, then concludes: "Let them [the Irish Protestants] thus live and testify, with one heart and one voice, the Gospel of the grace of God, and every papist within these four seas will soon acknowledge the truth as it is in Jesus."[3] One may ignore, for our purposes here, Wesley's typical anti-Roman prejudices, and still recognize that his real point applies as much, now as then, to us and our notions of evangelism: *Christianity is spread by Christians*—and rather more by their lives than by their lips!

Wesley knew—and we need to learn—that evangelism depends on preaching only in part. He was a great preacher (even if not as much of a "rouser" as legend has it) but this, by' itself, was not enough. Evangelism also depends on organization but only *in part* (Wesley was good at organization, too, with a ridiculously small and generally incompetent staff [it was too bad that it was not very competent but the Lord's mercy that it was small!]). But the real business of the Methodist revival was carried on *by the Methodist people,* under the guidance of the Holy Spirit—by *very ordinary people* (as far as human values go)—more often in Mr. Wesley's absence than presence. There'd have been no Wesleyan Revival without Wesley—that's for sure—but it is equally true that without that strange army of Christ's martyrs and servants that he managed to raise up, *to love God and to serve humankind* for the love of Christ, his revival would have been "a rope of sand," like so many others, before and since.

Odd, isn't it, to see an evangelist depending so heavily on the Holy Spirit, not only in theory (we *all* do that) but in practice as well! There was, to begin with, Wesley's understanding of the Spirit's mediation of "preventing" grace—and this means that evangelists must presume on the Spirit's initiatives *before* their words can be heard. Otherwise, the evangelist is tempted to turn to gimmicks and pious tricks. There was his belief in the Holy Spirit's salvific activity "among the heathen"—all those among them who fear God and live by the highest and best that he has revealed to them (through the agency of his universal Logos). There was his view of the Holy Spirit in the church, building it into a spiritual, sacramental community. Indeed, in Wesleyan terms, it is the Holy Spirit who is himself the Divine Evangelist, enabling us in our evangelizing insofar as we are truly open to *his* leading. And this means that evangelism is always both a message *and* a lifestyle—the Word made flesh, the Word made audible and credible, the Word made visible and winsome, in whatever format any actual situation calls for.

There will be those, here and elsewhere, who will assess this Convocation and Consultation by its speeches, pronouncements and headlines—by the spiritual "highs" that many of us will experience in the course of our pilgrim encounters in this Holy Land. But the world will judge us differently, and so will I. *Its* real question (and mine) is how many of us will leave here more deeply resolved and more adequately prepared to evangelize in and through our lifestyles as well as our messages—aflame with a renewed commitment to evangelize for Christ, as *his* martyrs and servants, wherever and however we can make a difference, or even hope to.

Some of these reflections may be silhouetted more clearly by listing some eight "uncheerful theses" that have been forming in my mind in the course of my reflections on this event and on this particular "fullness of time." These theses are negatively phrased but, obviously, each one has a positive counterpoint and I hope that these will occur to you as you hear and (I hope) ponder them. They are, one might say, "Outler's laws of ecclesiastical polity"—and are, of course, subject to existential interpretation:

1. An unconverted church is unlikely to convert the world.
the world.
2. A church bent on survival will not survive—nor does it deserve to.

3. A church obsessed by secular ideologies will never understand its inability to distinguish between the substance and the forms of true religion.

4. A church that mirrors the world in its own power structures will never impress that world with its *idealistic* pronouncements.

5. A church organized like a pyramid bears down hardest on those at its base.

6. A church that defines itself by tradition is headed toward self-chosen irrelevance.

7. A church that defines itself by "modernity" is headed toward uncomprehended failure.

8. A church that lives by the slogan will die by it, too.

Why, then, *have* we come here, and what will be the lasting significance of this event, if any? How far are we prepared even now—right now—to be re-formed and re-newed—in *our* repentance and in *our* commitments to Christ's true Lordship in the world, in *our* determination to enthrone him as liberator of the unfree, as Lord of *our* consciences and of the collective consciences in our several countries, as the head of a new humanity that really can function as his body? Are *these* the driving passions of our lives and are they, in turn, led captive to Christ's will and his spirit? How much of our evangel can others recognize in *our* lifestyles, in *our* active involvements in the truly Christian causes in the world? And are we really facing the fact that if we leave here without some such newness of insight and urgency, then the chief beneficiaries of this gathering will have been *the tourist business?*

What, then, will be the fruitage of this week in all those various places whence we *return*, whence we are sent as Christ's martyrs and humanity's servants? For until we have done all we can to make the Word of God audible, visible and winsome, then that world God loves so much will still have been betrayed, by us and all the others who bear Christ's holy name. For this is evangelism: not only to proclaim and argue and organize, or to play the numbers game (either way) but to walk and work in the world as heralds and placards of Christ (reconciled reconcilers, servants whose joy in service helps those whose service has been joyless to "see Jesus," as the One who came not to be ministered unto but to minister and to give his life for their redemption!). In this spirit, I ask you to join with me in a closing prayer for ourselves in these days, and for all Christians everywhere.

Give us, we pray thee, O God our Father, more Christians who feel their belonging, each to the other and to thee; more Christians who mediate thy healing love to all in pain, thy liberating love to all in bondage, thy hope-sustaining love to all in despair. Give us more Christians who will stand up and speak out, in accordance with their truest perceptions of thy gospel. Grant us, we pray thee, a bounteous inflooding of thy grace, a new strange warming of our own hearts by thy Holy Spirit—that we may experience anew and at an ever deeper level thy pardoning mercy, thine enabling power. But help us also, even as we pray for thy good gifts, to be ready to accept the tasks that come with each of them—and to know that any answer to such prayers of ours begins with our own willingness to be renewed in our covenant with thee: the covenant of outreach and service to a world in travail. All this we pray, in faith and hope, and in the name of Jesus who walked the Via Dolorosa long ago—and who still does, till thy kingdom shall come and thy will shall be done even on this aching earth as always it is done in heaven. And for these days and nights together, and for thy blessings upon them and us, we give thee thanks and glory—honor, majesty and dominion. Amen and Amen!

---

1. *The Spiritual Quixote* (1767), I, 55.
2. *Works*, X, 130.
3. Ibid., 133.

The Persuasions
of the Gospel

We are to think together concerning the most crucial
question for evangelism in our time—of any time. It is
the question as to what motive we shall appeal in
winning men and women to Christian discipleship. We
read that early in Jesus' ministry he faced the issue in
his so-called temptation experiences. Shall men become
Christians that they may have bread? Shall Christian
discipleship be associated with the power to work
wonders? Shall the final authority be a lordly rule over
men? One of the most pitiful sights in spiritual
experience is asking persons to do right things for the
wrong reason.

Now many of the grounds on which our forefathers
made disciples are no longer open to us. The appeal to
hell would not move most of our contemporaries.
Perhaps there is a hell for wrongdoers when our earthly
course is run, but most people of the twentieth century
do not believe so strongly enough to change their ways.
The appeal to worldly reward with which time-honored
evangelism took many a trick has little attraction. The
way of force is not open to us. Acknowledge that much
of the conquest of the Western world had force as an
ingredient, from the conversion of Constantine and later
the Franks in the fifth century. For many years it has
had no standing.

65

The chief persuasion for the gospel, historically and where the evangelism has been authentic, has been Christ himself. Through him millions of individuals have been transformed from worldly ways to that life which is life. Through him movements have been set in motion that have at least headed society in the direction of better things—in politics, in the production and distribution of goods, in healing the diseases of the body, in the relations between races and nations. Behind his teachings was a moral quality, and power to inspire—a strength that no other has been able to match. His coming has changed the currents of the world.

He is the source of the great advances that the Christian faith has made. Whenever he has been made the center of Christian aspiration there has been an increase in power, in appeal, in victory. Whenever he has been minimized, where he has been relegated to the fringes, the life of Christianity has waned, and the expression of it in the church has declined. He was responsible for the vast release of religious energy in the first century, unequalled in the history of our race. His conception of forgiveness was Luther's strength. Jesus Christ is the greatest force in human history for the shaping of character.

But mere calling on Christ does not guarantee a Christian state of affairs, for Christ has often been used for non-Christian purposes. He has often been looked on as the sanction for war. In the Middle Ages his name was invoked to cause Christians to fight against non-Christians and heretics. To criticize the "free enterprise" system is, in many minds, a repudiation of Christ. He is said to be against birth control. His universalism has been lauded, but its implications for the racial issue have not been applied. And democracy, defined as the opinion of the majority, has been looked on as the exemplification of Christian politics.

What is there in Christ that may be appealed to for the making of disciples? That is our theme. Let me mention three conceptions of him that are available to the evangelist.

66

First of all, he is *the divine-human ideal.* In quality he is what God is, infinitely, and what man ought to be. First of all was his sheer moral goodness. Whether he was wonder-worker, teacher, or a magnetic and luminous personality, his excellence judged by enlightened conscience stands the test. He did the things that a right-minded person does, and left undone the things that the truly upright condemns as unworthy. There was in him a total lack of concern for self. As the scripture tells us, "he loved us and gave himself for us." For our sakes he became poor. He demanded that the strong bear the burdens of the weak, because, as Paul put it, "he pleased not himself." His name was sympathy. In all our afflictions he was afflicted. He was touched with a feeling for our infirmities. He knew our frame and remembered that we are dust. His first sermons announced that he had come to preach good tidings to the poor. He possessed an esteem for woman that was not the rule in his generation. He made a hated Samaritan the hero of one of his greatest parables. He had a message for the world's unsuccessful.

He dedicated his life to his heavenly Father's purposes. He was a man of prayer, and at all the high points of his life his knee was bent to the will of God. He taught men that they ought always to pray and not faint. When at last he died in ignominy it was that the Father's will might be done. He endured the cross, despising shame, with a prayer for his enemies and a committal to God.

He had a majestic and towering personality which evoked admiration and devotion. A living evangelism in our time will repeat the story of Jesus Christ, painting him in such colors that he draws thoughtful and aspiring persons everywhere.

I am fully aware that there is an influential strain of New Testament study which says that we do not have enough material to present a life of Christ. Indeed, there is not enough to write a biography of the Master in the most elemental sense. And a good case for the point can be made, as Rudolf Bultmann has pointed out. And granted that we don't have much material on how Jesus looked, what he wore, what kind of house he lived in, and what he did on Monday mornings, or how he passed the sequence of his days. But of no other figure of antiquity do we know so much that is crucial for life—how he treated the people who rubbed elbows with him, the qualities of his thought, the modes of his expression, the basic beliefs on which he built his life, what he did and was done to him, and his impression on the people who knew him best. We may not have material for a *life* of Christ, but we possess a rich portrait.

The ideal is still one of the most potent influences of human experience. All action is initiated, governed, and carried to its goal by a mental picture of the good. Nowhere in man is there any pursuit, any achievement, any experience, any desire or expectation, apart from the presence and might of the ideal. The ideal of victory causes armies to march. The ideal of what is truly good determines the direction in which the will shall act. The ideal sustains and carries a person to his/her goal. As the apostle Paul remarks concerning his experience at Damascus: "I was not disobedient to the heavenly vision." An ideal controlling the mind creates character. The ideal inspires individuals to achievement as our Lord at his baptism and Isaiah in the temple. The ideal, seriously entertained, keeps us growing. The vision of the ideal renews people when they fail. And finally, the ideal transforms the world. The idealistic pioneer, dissatisfied with the world as it stands and entertaining a vision of the better future, is the real artificer of the world. A first task of an evangelist is to present Jesus Christ in his ideal character. Everywhere and always the vision of the good moves the will.

Many years ago a young man emigrated from Aberdeen, Scotland to America. Though he never acquired a high school or preparatory diploma, Charles Eliot, a famous president of Harvard, admitted him to that school as a special student. By the end of his first year he was admitted to the regular class because of the brilliance of his work. He continued his study and this boy, without a high school diploma, finished Harvard with *summa cum laude* honors, and a promise from Eliot that he would find the money to support him in graduate study with a hint and more that he would be appointed to Josiah Royce's chair when he retired. But he chose to go into the ministry. Before many years were spent as a minister, however, he confessed that he had run out of anything to preach about, and with it had come an almost giving up of the worth of preaching. In that extremity he resolved that for thirty minutes each morning he would read a passage from the Gospels, imagining that he (Gordon) were at the scene the Testament related. He considered each scene especially from its ideal side. He looked on the glimpses of childhood, full of wonder and beauty. He saw him at his baptism, receiving his commission. He listened to his teachings, his parables. He went with him on errands of mercy. He went with him to prayer and then back with him to the solemn business of living. He stayed with him as the clouds of opposition grew blacker and blacker. Finally, he saw him apprehended and tired, yet with comprehension of his plight he had compassion for those who condemned and crucified him. During this experience his congregation noticed a different note in his preaching. Gordon himself felt a greater satisfaction. At last he said that he could say with any of the apostles, "I, too, have seen the Lord." Soon thereafter he was called to Old South Church in Boston, where for forty-two years he preached with increasing power to one of the most distinguished Christian congregations in America. It witnesses to the power of the vision of the Christian ideal as seen in Jesus Christ.

In the second place, we may present Christ as *Redeemer*. Mere idealism is futile. Example, even divine-human example, is not enough. Some of the rabbis in Jesus' time taught things approximately the same in content as Jesus. But nothing happened. He declared sins forgiven, and they were forgiven. Paralyzed men rose to their feet and walked. C. H. Dodd, the famed interpreter of the New Testament, has a phrase, "the moral incompetence of human nature." We can appreciate the ideal and envision what might happen to us if we were to realize it, but we are not able to achieve it. The ideal is too high, we cannot attain unto it. Hence, we are encompassed by evil. We can understand what Mark Twain was referring to when he said that after he had read the morning paper, he always prayed for the damnation of the human race.

When Christ was here he had the power to minister to this moral incompetence of human nature. He came, sent by God, to seek and to save the lost, and he did it. He saved Zacchaeus from his flinty greed. Assuming that his parables are transcriptions of experience, he saved a penitent publican. He saved those who were lost to guidance, symbolized by the lost sheep. He saved those lost to usefulness, which the lost coin reminds us. He saved a wayward boy to loving companionship, the prodigal son. He told a thief dying on a nearby cross that he would not go out into extinction but would be with him in Paradise. The Book of Revelation pictures him, no less than twenty-nine times, as the Lamb of God that takes away the sins of the world.

And he still saves us from the things that ruin our lives. The evangelist's motive is to show that that is possible yet. The annals of Christianity are full of accounts of persons lifted by the Christian faith out of mediocrity into extraordinary beauty. Every disaster, private or social, reveals people who have found resources to meet their troubles not only with fortitude but with triumphant joy; in the midst of stress they have found peace. Christ uses Alcoholics Anonymous to break the grip of liquor. Persons in the Christian community, now models of gentility, confess how Christ took away their tempers. Hatred of men of other races has vanished as Christ took over. Fear, one of the most widespread contemporary maladies, can be overthrown by faith in One who can do all things by his strengthening. Many a Methodist church would be aghast to hear an old-fashioned gospel sermon on what

Christ can do for our ills. But they would be helped to the point of discipleship if it were done well.

Now, this appeal to the saving power of Christ involves for us the right use of the cross of Christ. Christ's pouring out of his death-blood is a moving symbol in itself. But sometimes its strength for thinking people has been reduced by its association with irrational, if not immoral, notions of calvary. We have indulged in a sacramentalism, which seems to teach that the cross is but a cosmic blood transfusion that works independently of the attitude of the believer. In the same class of moral and rational wrongness is a substitutionary theory which acquiesces in the punishment of the innocent in place of the guilty. "Jesus paid it all." Why, then asks the unwashed, should we have anything really to do? Such theology will serve to make Christians, but hardly in a valid way.

What the cross says to thoughtful Christians is that evil is to be redeemed only as men and women are willing to suffer pain or loss—symbolized by the life-blood. Many years ago I heard Henry Howard, a member of the Australian Methodist Church, later to have a second ministry at the First Presbyterian Church, New York City. He was preaching, as I remember, on the text, "Without the shedding of blood, there is no remission of sins." He recalled how he had once seen on the prairies of his native land a great hawk attack a prairie hen and her brood. As soon as the hawk appeared high overhead the mother sent out an air raid alarm and her chicks came running to find cover beneath her wings. The preacher then described with vividness how the hawk attacked, with the awesomeness of a dive-bomber on an open city. The little mother took an awful wounding from the marauder's talons, but she fought back as best she could. And finally the hawk made off. When it had gone the fluffy little chicks came out from the protecting wings, but Dr. Howard noted that with each of them there was a spot of red on the fluffy down. "Without the shedding of blood" there was no remission of their plight. And so, along with the

71

preaching of Christ as Savior, we must present the fact that is to be achieved by no slick theological sleight-of-hand, or psychological magic, but is to carry with it sacrifice by us, as well as by the Redeemer.

Finally, our evangelism should proclaim him not only as the ideal, and the Savior, but as *victor*. For such he was when he was here. The conviction he gave when he was in our midst was of a man of power—power over men, most of all. He called men to his discipleship, and straightway they left their nets and followed him. He had power over minds in his teaching: "they were astonished at his teaching." He had power over persons—often we read that they did not understand one of his sayings "and they were afraid to ask him." And when he found the thieves desecrating the temple he became "the Christ of the whip," and they fled before him. So impressive was his following that they had to take him by stealth. He had power over disease. He had power over demons and drove them out. And when we reach the end of his life, a pagan Roman centurion of the execution detail calls him a son of God. And when an unknown writer strives to rally a wavering church in the Book of Revelation, it is with the picture of a majestic figure standing in the midst of seven golden candlesticks. He is King of kings, Lord of lords.

Finally, he was victor over death. His resurrection is the pivotal fact of the New Testament. There is nothing more certain than that the Master was put to death by the military. The disciples had seen it with their own eyes. They went back to their boats concerned that the Christian movement was over. "We trusted," they said, "that it had been he who should have redeemed Israel." Their hopes were buried in Joseph's tomb.

And just as certain is the fact that in three days they were changed men. They sprang upon the world with the boldness of lions. They went everywhere proclaiming a risen Lord. And all of those early disciples—with the possible exception of two—sealed their conviction with their lifeblood. Suppose that instead of our presenting Christ as a pure, good man, an idealist for whom the powers of this world were too much, we were to offer him as one who was on top of every circumstance he met, death not excepted. Wouldn't our evangelism have an impact not unlike that of the first days?

In the long run, success in the world of the spirit, as well as in the world of common affairs, flows to victory. One of the things that military historians are saying concerning World War II, as true of one side as another, is that calling on troops to fight with "their backs to the wall" is rarely effective in stiffening their spine. It is confidence in victory that finally achieves the victory. History knows few victories through despair. As confidence in their Lord's resurrection sent the first generation out into an unfriendly world with *élan* that brought victory, I am convinced that when our morale, as followers of a Lord who won, is grounded in justifiable hope, Christianity will come back.

Our task is to call a moratorium on our pessimism. No, I am not preaching that we are to make ourselves believe an untruth. Let us recognize that one cannot be both a pessimist and an evangelist. But we can act as we would if we knew Christ were to win, and as the great text from John has it, "If any man will do his will, he shall know of the doctrine whether it be of God." When it looked as though defeat were inevitable, the prophet Jeremiah, a prophet often named as most like Christ in temperament in the Old Testament, bought a plot of land in the village of Anathoth just to show his people the depth of his conviction that at last the Lord would prevail. He acted as though he followed a victor. I believe that such faith in the triumph of God, despite our generation's discouragements, the perplexities of social action, and despite the inertness, shallowness, and wavering resolve of so many Christians, will win again.

Tarry in Jerusalem

I began preaching in the streets of Madras, my home city in India. When you preach in the streets and on street corners, you have to have a strong feeling of something that compels you from within to tell the truth. I remember once when I was coming home with some bags of groceries, a compulsion came upon me, so I set the bags down and began to sing. The thing that I do to stop people is to sing! You don't have to have a great voice to stop people. The very fact you have the daring to sing will stop them, and once you have their attention fixed even momentarily, you need to give out the word as quickly as you can before their interest fails. And you've got to be ready to be countered with questions. It is not the sedate Sunday morning congregation; it is people, virile and active.

There are great similarities between this gathering in Jerusalem and a street corner crowd in Madras. We are here waiting. We are here saying, "If you've got it, give it out." We are saying, "We have been waiting for a moment of commitment and if now is the moment, tell us." But I'm afraid of one thing: There is a certain amount of preplanned structure in this gathering which is absolutely lacking in a street corner meeting, and it can take us into that same lethargy that can happen at a Sunday morning service in any given church.

75

Simplicity was the word that came to simple people on the shepherd's field. They were poor people. God started with them. He is still a God who speaks to simple people in simple tones. If you sense in my proclamation too much simplicity, it is because I'm a simple man.

> Then opened he their understanding, that they might understand the scriptures,
> And said unto them, Thus it is written, and thus it behoved Christ to suffer, and to rise from the dead the third day:
> And that repentance and remission of sins should be preached in his name among all nations, beginning at Jerusalem.
> And ye are witnesses of these things.
> And, behold, I send the promise of my Father upon you: but tarry ye in the city of Jerusalem, until ye be endued with power from on high.
>
> [Luke 24:45–49]

Earlier, in the nineteenth chapter, Luke speaks about a rising feeling of expectation among the disciples. Jesus was going to Jerusalem, and the people began to feel that the kingdom of God would be a reality. But Jesus had to tell them in simple terms, in parabolic language, that such an anticipation would not be immediately fulfilled. He spoke about being occupied while waiting.

I will never forget a book whose chief character is Rip Van Winkle, a man who succeeded in sleeping through a whole revolution, a man who was so detached that he woke up after all the action was over. It is sometimes possible by our own willfulness to be withdrawn because we are threatened by change—*quick* change—that we see all around us.

Riding in a taxi from Tel Aviv to Jerusalem, the man who was with me said, "It is a perplexing world, is it not? You cannot find any answers. Nobody seems to be able to give an answer." The temptation was to say, "Why get entangled in the perplexity? Let me withdraw, let me protect myself," and then to sleep comfortably through the revolution. But it's impossible to do so because the Master has told us, "I have left you behind in order that you may be involved, that you may be involved while you wait." It is an active waiting process.

An Indian would authenticate religious experience on the basis of two factors: one called *torisina*, or "the vision"; the second, *onboa*, or "the experience." The two go together. In fact, this is not strange to Pauline theology. Paul spoke about the eyes of our hearts being opened. In the Ephesian episode (1:18) we are told that God may enlighten the eyes of our hearts. It is something that is deep within. It is something that is in the secrecy of the individual. There is a vision which God gives, and this vision is given as a common element to every believer. What is this vision? When Jesus called his disciples he endued them personally with this power. If we read the parable, we shall find that he called them one by one and gave the charge that entrusted the vision personally to each of them. This vision is given personally and yet knowledgeably. When Jesus was born, the people who were responsible for naming him said, "You will call his name Jesus." Why? Because he will save people. From what? From their sins. The name of Jesus seems miraculously to help people think about the forgiveness that God grants them.

We live in a sin-riddled world. In a world in which the word *sin* is no longer theory but an absolute, implicit, practical measure, the most necessary proclamation is, "There is forgiveness, there is hope for beginning." How many pastors have sat down and talked with people into the wee hours of the morning where the implicit question was, "Is there a hope for me to begin all over again? Is there another chance for me?" There was a man who went into the temple the day King Uzziah died (Isaiah 6). He came out of a perplexed world. He was full of perplexity, also. The only place he could go was to where there could be hope from beyond. The whole temple was full of his presence. The train of the Lord filled the temple and then the vision began to speak. I often ask myself, "How would I tell a person in the interior of India what the vast ocean is like?" Suppose I go into a village and say, "Out in Madras, we've got a big beach and a tremendous ocean that extends miles and miles and miles." He has never seen that much water, so he begins to ask, "Is it as big as the well in my backyard?" Then I scratch my head and think, Where do I begin? Suppose I say, "It's a hundred million wells put together." Who has seen the figure *one hundred million* in anything more than *one* followed by several zeroes? We talk about the multiplied millions of humanity all over the world, yet how many of us have seen one million human beings at one time together? None of us. There are several things that are known only in terms of mathematical figures whose magnitude we will never understand until the small world we know is filled. Then God somehow says, "This is how I fill the rest of the world, also."

So God took him into the temple, filled the temple with his presence, and then Isaiah was prepared to say, "The whole earth is full of his glory. I thought everything was gone. I thought man had no possibility of redemption. Here the whole earth is full of his glory and God is filling every inch of his creation. He has not given up. He is very much in action."

Where does this all begin? It begins with one's acknowledgment of the Lord. Corruption, debauchery, prejudices, pride—every one of these things is filled with the *me*, always *me*. I must acknowledge that I am a man of unclean lips and that I live among people with unclean lips. Then God can begin to do something with me. With such an awareness, then and only then, can one begin to say, "He has endued me; he has given me a commonality that is open to all persons, if they would only see it." Then one's authority no longer rests within one's self. Meaning for existence is not sought merely with one's own intellect or within one's own emotions

78

or will. The self is transcended and meaning is found in something far more than the self. Such a person is truly liberated and entrusted by God with something that all mankind is seeking!

Jesus Christ constantly keeps us moving and says, "I have committed into your hands this tremendous charge. Now will you occupy yourselves because I'm coming back one day and I'm going to ask you what you did with it?"

The call of the altar has touched us. Our sins are forgiven. Our guilt is removed. Whom shall we thank? And then the other question, Who will go? For even if we make the choice the final point of the answer is in our will. Will we go?

Here my Lord, send me!

The angel cried, "Holy, holy, holy is the Lord of hosts." And what is our immediate concept of holiness? We got together a group of college youth in our church and asked them, "What is holiness?" They said, "Purity." I said, "What is purity?" They said, "It is a clean white shirt which has not been touched with any speck." That is our concept of purity, isn't it? If that is the concept of purity we have, then we must constantly be afraid that something is going to contaminate us. Not so with the purity and holiness of God. It is an aggressive holiness. It contaminates sin. Sin cannot stand in God's presence. When God was there and the eyes of the prophet were opened, the first thing he said was, "I am a man with unclean lips." Nobody preached a sermon to him! There was no evangelist present because there was no need for one! If we see the holiness of God, the next thing that happens is that it seeks to contaminate us.

Simon Peter met Jesus along the Sea of Galilee. Jesus did not preach a sermon to him, but Simon came and fell down at his feet and said, "Depart from me. I'm a sinful man." "Who told you about your sinfulness?" replied Jesus. Nobody needed to. Jesus put out his hand and touched him. The help Jesus offered flowed through him. This is the holiness that God is talking

79

about. This is the kind of involvement into which God is inviting each of us!

Recall the woman who came up behind Jesus in the press of a crowd and touched him. Jesus turned to Simon and said, "Someone has touched me." Simon said, "There are so many people in this crowd that everybody is touching you." But Jesus said, "It was a different kind of touch. Something has flown out of me and someone who has been sick has now been healed." The woman came trembling and said, "Yes, Lord, that's right. I've been healed." It is this kind of authentication that God gives to you and me! The beginning comes when the eyes of our hearts are opened and we know that God's holiness is contagious.

Is not the cross the deepest revelation of this holiness of God? Is not the cross God's statement that he is in agony until what to be *is*? If the eyes of our hearts are open, then how can we say that we have not seen this? Is this not the common investment of each of us here who would say, "He has forgiven me"? "If we confess our sins, he is faithful and just to forgive us our sins, and to cleanse us from all unrighteousness" (1 John 1:9).

There was a little girl who went to her room to go to bed. Her mother tucked her into bed and went to her own room to sleep. Not long afterward, the girl rolled off the bed and with a thud fell onto the floor. Her mother came in, picked her up, comforted her, and put her back in the bed again. It happened a second time and a third time. This time the mother sat with her child and said, "Honey, why is it that you're rolling off the bed so frequently tonight?" The little girl in sleepy wisdom replied, "Mommy, I went to sleep too close to the point where I got in, and one little turn and I'm off the bed." Too many of us have gone to sleep too close to the point where we got in. There are not many here who would refuse to say, "Yes, God has forgiven me; he has cleansed me; he has made me whole; he has contaminated me in the right sense of the word." We will praise him for that. But we've gone to sleep too close to the point where we got in! Every little turn and we are off the bed again, preoccupied with ourselves. We can, in a very real sense, sleep through a revolution!

Forgiveness and cleansing are like two doors in one doorway. They open in order to permit entrance into a larger life. A little four-year-old boy was asked, "What are doors for?" And he said very readily, "They are meant to keep little boys out." Doors can keep people out, but doors are also entrances. Jesus said, "I am the door. If you want to enter in, you must pass through me. I'm not here to keep you out. I'm here to show you how to get in." The twin doors are forgiveness and cleansing but there is a whole lifestyle into which God is inviting each of us.

What are the main accents of this lifestyle? Three little words: life, love, and light. Let me begin with the word *life*. John calls it *eternal life*. "He that hath the Son, hath life; and he that hath not the Son of God hath not life" (1 John 5:12). There can be no more simple statement than that. What kind of life is this? This is eternal life. What do we mean by *eternal?* It is indestructible. What do we mean by *indestructible?* Things of this common living can no longer corrode this life. It does not crumble under pressure! It stands up to it because it is the life of the living God. It is his life lived in and through us.

I am a veterinarian. During the process of that kind of an education, they taught me something about animal genetics. Some of you here have heard the word *aleal.* When two chromosomes mix together there is a dominant aleal and there is a recessive aleal. They do not inhibit each other but they work with each other. The dominant aleal, whichever parent may contribute that, determines the color of the hair, the color of the eyes, the structure of the body. Many things are determined by the dominant aleal, but the recessive aleal accepts the dictation of the dominant aleal so that through the interaction of two—one willing, the other dictating—the life that emerges takes shape. The same thing happens in the life of an individual within whom Jesus Christ is the ruling, final authority. I become the recessive aleal; he becomes the dominant aleal. He dictates to me the shape my life will take. It is his life lived through me. Because it is God's life, it is indestructible life!

There is another word: *love*. John says, "We love him because he first loved us" (1 John 4:19). C.S. Lewis, that brilliant, clear-thinking Englishman calls it "four loves" in a little book by that same title. "Need love" is the first love of which all of us are aware. There is not a living person but who has felt it. "Need love" has strange ways of expressing itself. Empty as I am, I go to another emptier than myself expecting my bucket to be filled, but the person answers, "I was expecting you to fill *my* bucket!" We hold out our buckets to one another, both saying that we are empty—each waiting to be filled by the other!

There was a woman who met Christ at the village well. He told her, "Come to me. I'll give you water so that you will never thirst again." O Lord, fill my bucket! It's empty! In my home, in my relationship to my community—wherever I need to express myself well, I find my emptiness staring at me. O God, where can I go! Fill my cup, O Lord. I'm holding it up to you. Unless you fill it, I am empty. Where can I find such love, except in you?

A lawyer came to Jesus and questioned him. The Master spoke in simple terms. A Samaritan was beaten up by robbers and ignored. Religious people were walking around him. There were three different laws operating there. The first was the "law of the jungle." The bandits got what they wanted by brute force, but they really got nothing. The second was the "law of diplomacy." We of the church are highly skilled in this art. We forever give reasons and rationalizations to get what we want but the very rationalizing process stares back at us and tells us that we don't have what we think you have! Then came the third person. He used the "law of love." He was a Samaritan—a most nonreligious example, and yet how the law of love worked in him. He picked up the irreconcilable—the distinction of race—and said, "I'll put you to flight!" He ignored the irresistible temptation of retaliation and hatred and said, "I'll put you to flight!" He chose the unrepayable—a good turn not to be rewarded—and said, "I'll do it!" And Paul would say, "For the law of the Spirit of life in Christ Jesus hath made me free from the law of sin and of death" (Rom. 8:2). It is still the spirit of Christ. The result of love is that it casts out fear. If we do not know this, we go to sleep too close to the place where we got in.

The third word is *light*. The joy of walking with God is walking in the light, according to John. If we obey what God has to tell us, then our fellowship with him is unbroken. How can a Christian amount to anything when fellowship with the Creator is broken? "But if we walk in the light, as he is in the light we have fellowship one with another" (1 John 1:7) and with God. John says that it is our desire to have fellowship with one another because our fellowship is with Jesus Christ. Walking in the light. What does it mean? Let me again use a biblical example. Two men were beaten up for proclaiming the truth about Jesus Christ—Paul and Silas. They were locked up inside a prison, but still they sang. The foundation of the prison began to shake. But the singing did not convince the jailer. The jailer was convinced when Paul called out and said, "Listen, don't hurt yourself! We are not using any shortcuts in this world. Just because the door is open, we're not going to run away from here. Our destiny is in the hands of the living God and we will follow his rule, his goal, his light." What a message in a day like this! Who walks in the light? It is the person who refuses to take the temptation of a shortcut. When those called by the name Jesus refuse to do this, then the world will stand up and say, "Let me also find him."

In the compartment of a passenger train in India, an elderly grandmother was trying to get out. The train had stopped in such a place that her compartment was beyond the platform so that it was difficult for her to step down. She stood there not knowing how to get out.

Everybody began to give advice to her. Someone said, "Just step lower, step down a little, and you'll reach it. You're doing all right." But nobody did anything. There was a Christian in that compartment. Someone began to move within his heart and said, "Do something about the situation." So he got up, then went down on all fours where the steps ended and said, "Mother, step on me." The old lady stepped on him and got off. The car blew its whistle and the Christian got back into the compartment. There was stillness and then somebody said, "He must be a Christian." If this is not true of us we go to sleep too close to the place where we got in.

I have spoken about the common vision which God gives, about the common experience that God grants to you and me—to have the light, to walk in the light, and to love. And now, let me go to the final statement—the common endowment which God gives. Tarry until you are endued with power (Luke 24:49). Whose power? God's power!

In Romans 8, there are three groanings that we read about. The first is the groaning of all creation. I think we do not have to talk about it much. We have all sensed it and know it. Creation groans because there is a new order waiting to be born and it's coming through. Then there is the groaning of the children of God—those who know, as their eyes are opened, those who are experienced in smaller or larger measure. They groan because what is now and what is yet to be seem to be two irreconcilable things. They say, "God, what I've tasted begs for more; give it to me!" And there is a deep groaning. I think most of us, or some of us, have known this. But the Bible doesn't leave the groaning merely to creation and to man. The Bible says also that there is one who groans—the Holy Spirit. A long time ago, the Holy Spirit groaned within the heart of Wilberforce and things began to happen. A long time ago the Holy Spirit began to groan in the heart of Lord Shaftesbury and things began to happen. Not too long ago the Holy Spirit began to groan in the heart of a man called Sadasundra Singh and things began to happen in my

84

country! Can he groan again? Will he groan in your heart and mine? Except for this function of the Holy Spirit, there is no mission at all. Except for this sensitivity that the Spirit gives to us, there is no progress, no direction! Praise God! He is a common element given to you and me.

E. Stanley Jones is a magic name in India; to me it is the name of a guru. E. Stanley Jones spoke about his experience of being filled with the Holy Spirit. He told how God spoke to him and said, "Stanley, will you give me your all as I give you my all?" And Jones says, "I knelt down and I asked God, 'Is it that simple?' " And God said, "Yes, it is simple." And then, without hesitation, Dr. Jones said, "I turned to God and said, 'I close the ball game, you got me.' " And God turned around and told him, "All right, Stanley, you got me. Get up; move." E. Stanley Jones walked up and down the little room, struggling. The doubts of the devil began to plague him and he said, "With my two hands, I push the doubts of the devil away." And then God asked him, "Stanley, do you believe in your emotions or do you believe in my word?" That settled it. He said, "Yes, Lord, I believe." At that moment Dr. Jones said, "Floodtides of blessing from heaven descended on me that I had to finally say, 'Hold it, Lord, I can't take it anymore.' " The rest is history, isn't it? The touch is at that point. Will you give me your *all*?

Love conquers fear. Fill my cup, Lord; get that fear out of me. I'm afraid to make the initial approach and yet I've got to communicate—time's running out. Get that fear out of me! In a world that is so busy, I want to get by and I've done so many things, and God, I've never been able to convince people about who you are. My lifestyle is influenced by others, not by you, Master. You're not my absolute. I've frozen myself; unfreeze me. "Tarry. I give you my Father's promise; it will not fail. Will you take it?"

Motivation
for Evangelism

The risen Christ spoke at length with his followers about the evangelization of the world, as is clearly shown in the five passages of the New Testament where he sends out his disciples to conquer the world (Matt. 28:18–20; Mark 16:15–18; Luke 24:46–49; John 20:21–23; Acts 1:7–8). This commission is threefold: (1) to bring forth the message; (2) to lead into faith; and (3) to make disciples. It all has to do with God's mighty works of salvation.

Traditionally, the concept of salvation has basically been used in two ways. It may mean "come into faith," but also "final salvation." In both cases the term expresses *God's* work for and in persons, when the fruits of Christ's life, death, and resurrection are appropriated and actualized in the lives of individual persons through the power of the Holy Spirit. Essentially, this means reestablishment of the broken relationship between a person and God, and its fulfillment in eternity. Thus a new life, a life of faith, comes into being—a life which may grow into holiness and fullness. Lately, however, the concept of salvation has been given a much wider content which also includes new interrelationships among people, expressed as justice, liberation, solidarity, and the like. The resultant confusion and uncertainty between the primary God-man relationship and the consequent man-to-man relationships opens the way for using the term in such a vague way that it becomes almost impossible to know clearly what is meant.

Something similar is being done to the concept of evangelism. It is often used now to include more or less the whole of Christian life and service, resulting in a similar vagueness and confusion as to what is actually meant. To avoid this, I shall make use of the clear definition given in the 1974 Lausanne declaration.

> To evangelize is to spread the good news that Jesus Christ died for our sins and was raised from the dead according to the Scriptures, and that as the reigning Lord he now offers the forgiveness of sins and the liberating gift of the Spirit to all who repent and believe. Our Christian presence in the world is indispensable to evangelism. . . . But evangelism itself is the proclamation of the historical, biblical Christ as Saviour and Lord, with a view to persuading people to come to him personally and so be reconciled to God. In issuing the gospel invitation we have no liberty to conceal the cost of discipleship. Jesus still calls all who would follow him to deny themselves, take up their cross, and identify themselves with his new community. The results of evangelism include obedience to Christ, incorporation into his church and responsible service in the world. (Par. 4)

Thus, evangelism means proclaiming the saving gospel of forgiveness of sins to all persons, by all means, at all times, and in all places. It is the will of our Lord that the message of his death, victorious resurrection, and love be brought to all people. The purpose is to lead persons to faith, to a personal relationship with Christ, and to the fellowship of forgiven sinners. This again must lead to discipleship if the new life is to live and grow. The believer is not only a person whom Christ has forgiven and given a new life, but a person ruled and used by him. The work of evangelism cannot be measured by how many there are who come into faith, but rather by how many become true disciples. Love of God must, as a consequence, lead to love of neighbor. This means being a witness of God's saving work in Christ. But it also means doing good to all—body and soul, struggling for love, justice, and freedom. The latter, however, should not in itself be seen as evangelism, but rather as its consequences. The life of faith must bring forth the fruits of faith or it will stagnate and become powerless. One of the basic expressions of John Wesley is the well-known phrase, "faith working through love." The love of God given to the believer becomes no less than the powerful dynamic and motivating source and means for the Christian's total life. This God-given love brings into being new attitudes and motivation, as well as new acts of love.

The driving force and motivation of the Christian's service to God and fellowman is, therefore, the love of God revealed in his heart. Nevertheless, this service has also another side. It may even function as what may be called preparatory evangelism. Serving the immediate needs of a person or group of persons may make the gospel of love and forgiveness more credible, thus preparing the way for repentance, forgiveness, and a new life in Jesus Christ. The objection may be raised that this is nothing but a cynical exploitation of people in need: "You believe, you eat!" Of course this is possible, but only if *believe* means formal adherence to certain doctrines or only formally becoming a Christian. The *motive* of the person who serves must be the love of God. The *purpose* must be to bring this new life in God to those who are served, and not simply to make institutional and formal gains in terms of adherents. Therefore, service in the world for the good of others is not identical with evangelism. But neither can it be severed apart from it. In terms of what is primary and must be given highest priority, these things cannot be seen as a chicken-and-egg question, where there is doubt about what comes first. We are *enabled* to love, because we have *received* God's forgiving love through Jesus Christ. "We love because he first loved us." Thus, the basic presupposition for a person's witness and service of God and man is to *know* Jesus Christ, not only to *know about* him. If we claim to go in the name of Jesus Christ, we had better know him first! On the other hand with regard to the persons to whom witness and service in Jesus Christ is directed, in terms of time, witness may come first, or service, or both may occur at the same time. In the evangelistic task, *service* to others alone does not suffice, since "faith comes from what is heard, and what is heard comes by the preaching of Christ" (Rom. 10:14–17). For the Christian, however, faith and service are both parts of the new life in Jesus Christ.

So far, we have attempted in some measure to define the task of evangelism as well as to point to some necessary presuppositions for it. But what is really the motivation for evangelism? Why evangelize? Sloganeering has become quite popular in our time. One such slogan which appears to be *in* at present is "the world sets the agenda." It seems plausible and reasonable, but is nevertheless false. *God* sets the agenda for the Christian. The world, the situation and circumstances can at most only influence *how* this agenda is carried out. *The primary and basic motivation* for evangelism is the fact that it is carried out *for Christ's sake and in his name* and not for the sake of persons. We have already pointed out that having received a new life in Jesus Christ as a forgiven sinner is the *sine qua non* of evangelism. The source of love and service, witness and living for neighbor is for the Christian God's love revealed in his heart through the Holy Spirit. The love of God compels us! No one is any longer regarded from a human point of view: "Therefore, if any one is in Christ, he is a new creation: the old has passed away, behold the new has come. All this is from God, who through Christ reconciled us to himself and gave us the ministry of reconciliation; ... entrusting to us the message of reconciliation. So we are ambassadors for Christ, God making his appeal through us"

(2 Cor. 5:14–21). Thus the Christian's service of reconciliation—whether that be reconciliation with God or among others—has its source, root, and deepest motivation in Jesus Christ. Witness and service are done for *his* sake, in *his* name, whatever the needs are of those to whom this witness and service are directed. The ultimate basis for the Christian's new life in its totality is God's love expressed in Jesus Christ. Christ's life, suffering, death, and resurrection have once for all provided the basic foundation for man's salvation in him. His atoning work provides the ground for the new creation, which is and must be existentially appropriated by and in man through the power of the Holy Spirit. Thus, the basic and primary *motivation* for evangelism must be understood as Christocentric and soteriological, rather than anthropocentric and humanistic. The greatest sin of modern man is that he makes himself the center and king of his life. To make man's needs the ultimate and primary motivation for evangelism would then be another expression of this man-centered and self-sufficient pride. It is also a question of commitment, but not only of commitment in general, nor primarily of commitment to the church, but to Jesus Christ. Finally, it is also a question of a commission. Christ said, "Go therefore and make disciples of all nations" (Matt. 28:19). And "repentance and forgiveness of sins should be preached in his name to all nations" (Luke 24:47).

Furthermore, evangelism is also motivated by the needs of persons in their total life. There is, however, a basic truth that must never be forgotten or neglected, namely, *man's greatest need is to be reconciled with God!* One may cater to the needs of others, whether that means securing food, shelter, health, freedom, justice, or many other things. One's basic motivation can be of many kinds: political, racial, economic, humanitarian, search for power, selfishness, compassion, or the like. Christians may do the same, but their basic motivation is the love of Christ. Unless the message "be reconciled to God" (2 Cor. 5:20) clearly reaches persons whom we seek to serve, then we have failed in our primary task as Christians. Only the Christian can offer Christ. Realizing that the love of God is a necessary presupposition for loving others, we must preach the gospel of forgiveness for all to all. In all we as Christians do, whether in social action or service or whatever it may be, bringing the message of salvation in Jesus Christ, fulfilling the ministry of reconciliation, must be the central and essential task. This is the essence of evangelism. It is necessary for God's sake as well as for man's sake. Other forms of Christian life and service are not thereby excluded, but first and primary things must have highest priority and be the underlying motive and goal in all we as Christians do or say. It has been argued that emphasis upon forgiveness and commitment to Jesus Christ has too often led to an introverted form of spiritual life, where responsibility for the world around us is largely nonexistent. But to draw the conclusion that working for commitment to Jesus Christ should therefore not be emphasized is equally wrong. We need to take the words of John Wesley seriously, when he says, "the right cure for misuse is not disuse, but the right use." *How* the Christian witness and service is carried out is to a large extent dependent upon the situation. Western man, with all his inner emptiness and a sense of meaninglessness, needs more than anything else to hear the simple words of Jesus Christ as Savior, whose love is offered to all who will receive. This so much the more because the problems of life in an affluent society are basically spiritual, not material. An increasing number seek to fill their lives with or find meaning in such things as occultism, spiritism, astrology, and various kinds of adapted Eastern mystical religions. But most of the people try to fill their lives with things. The constant longing for this or that, and then finally achieving it, appears to give some meaning to their lives, but not for long. This may also express itself in a hedonism where sensual satisfaction becomes a way of finding some meaning in life. But the result in either of these pursuits is too often total ennui. In another part of the world ministering to other needs, hunger, justice, freedom, and the like, may be most pressing and must be given the immediate attention. But even then the ultimate purpose and goal remains: to lead all persons to faith in Jesus Christ.

Lastly, evangelism may also be motivated by the needs of the individual Christian. Having received the new life of love in Jesus Christ, this new life demands being lived out in service to God and others. By receiving, one may become a new creation in Christ. By receiving, ordinarily through the means of grace, one is empowered to live a life of love in the Spirit. But such power is given *in order to* do something: We receive power in order that we may use it in witness and service. Power and love that are not used or lived out will end up in weakness and lovelessness. A Christian who refuses to be an ambassador for Christ, who neglects to witness about his forgiving love offered to all people, will find his spiritual power ebb away. Likewise, a spiritual life not lived out in service will also lose its power. Love of God must necessarily lead to love of humankind (1 John 4:20–21). In the same sense, the whole body of Christ, the living church, shall truly live *in* the world, though without being absorbed *by* it. It is fundamentally wrong to use such terms as *individual* or *collective* in connection with the believers and the body of Christ. The individual implies rejection of the collective; the collective absorbs and annihilates the individual. In the body of Christ, in the *communio sanctorum,* the *person* is fully affirmed as the body becomes one through the bond of the Holy Spirit, i.e., the bond of God's love revealed *in* us and *among* us. Therefore, the whole body of Christ will remain healthy and true only to the extent that it lives out its essential God-given nature, namely, a whole body in loving witness and service. The priesthood of all believers is not something optional to be exercised at will, but rather an essential and absolutely necessary function of the whole body of believers.

Why then evangelize?

For Christ's sake. He died for us. He receives the

sinner with forgiving love making him a new being. He commands us to go. To bring out this message is the primary task of the Christian.

For the sake of man. Man's greatest need is to be reconciled with God in order that he may be enabled to live a life of love.

For the sake of the individual Christian. The life of faith demands witness and service of God and man.

This is the greatest miracle: God has in his wisdom made it so that his message of salvation should be brought to humanity through people who themselves are forgiven sinners. He takes whatever we bring in our hands and makes it into a wonderful harvest in his kingdom.

In this sense may every Methodist be a true evangelist before God and man.

The Mission before Us

One of the main boards of our church has a very significant name. It is called the Board on Life and Mission of the Church. If we think for a moment about that name, we shall see that there is an intimate relationship between both terms. From a strictly logical, intellectual point of view, *life* is prior. First comes life, then *mission*. But logic reveals its serious limitations as soon as we turn the terms around and begin to think in such an affirmation as this: "Mission is the life of the church." Without mission, there is no life, no church. The church lives by its mission. Mission belongs to the very essence of the church. Life is already mission. Therefore, with regard to practical effects one cannot distinguish mission from life. Everything in the life of the church is or ought to be an expression of its mission. And anything that cannot be so needs to be called into question in the name of the Lord of the church. Therefore, in a sense everything that happens in a church is evangelism of a sort. It may be real evangelism or anti-evangelism, in which case there is a denial of the Lordship of Jesus Christ.

Not long ago a layman commented at a meeting: "What occurs is that the church does not seem to take off." We cannot deny that there is a deep crisis in the life of the church today. That this is the case in other

95

denominations as well, and that it is universal, is of no comfort at all. The important question here is: What does God want to tell us by means of the crisis? There is nothing to gain by sitting and lamenting over it. Nor can we step out of it by turning to ingenious techniques. The crisis is of a spiritual nature, and it is in that realm that it must be solved. Hence the question, What is God saying to us by means of the crisis? I am not saying, of course, that God sends the crisis. This may come because of our disobedience, or because we have ceased to listen to God and search for his guidance.

When we say that this crisis is spiritual in nature, we are not denying that it is institutional, organizational, educational, and the rest. What we mean by spiritual is that which is related to the Holy Spirit. Then the question is whether we have neglected the Spirit. Sometimes we have tried to substitute human activities, programs, organizations, plans and techniques for the work of the Holy Spirit. We have set up goals regarding the number of converts, as if Christians could be made to order. Or we have rested content with interesting others in the church or its activities but we have not been concerned whether they came into a vital encounter with the Holy Spirit. On the other hand we have sometimes neglected the Spirit in the name of the Spirit. We have mistaken the work of the Spirit for certain feelings. We have then tried to manipulate people's emotions by diverse psychological means. Who knows how much enthusiastic, pious, and fervent activities of evangelization must be reckoned under this heading? Many times our effort to change people's behavior so that they may conform to our ways of thinking, feeling, and acting is an expression of our lack of faith in the work and power of the Holy Spirit. We then tend to forget that the Spirit comes to meet us as whole persons—bodies, minds, and souls; emotion, intellect and will; at the conscious and subconscious levels—in order to bring us the reality of a love such as the one described in First Corinthians 13, a chapter about which it is far easier to sing praises than to incarnate in our life.

The church cannot take off by human means. None of our devices will do. What is needed is that we listen to what the Spirit says to the church. And after that, we should be faithful in our obedience. Until we recover the sense of being guided by the Spirit as was the primitive church, according to the Book of Acts, we will be unable to take off, and will remain grounded. This may seem impractical. The person who has never been prompted to do something he did not understand can be understood to share this opinion. But he who knows himself to have been taken by God to do what he did not expect to do or say will know that this can turn out to be the most practical thing upon earth. Our Christian mission, to say it in the most concise way I can, is *to proclaim the gospel.*

But what does it mean to proclaim the gospel today? What is the gospel? To try to answer this we can be led almost immediately into deep theological waters. John 3: 16, which is often quoted as the "simple" gospel, is not so simple after all. It begins with the assertion that God is, and goes on to the nature of God as love and as interested in the whole world. It says that God is a missionary, God who sent his Son Jesus Christ. That by itself speaks of the uniqueness of Christ and the uniqueness of his relationship to the Father. It speaks to us of a Person who cannot be locked within human categories, for he transcends them in an absolute fashion. And it speaks of faith as universally offered to "whosoever." It calls us to have faith in him, which puts us before the mystery of the cross and the redemption which is included in the "may not die but have eternal life." Surely there is enough there for volumes of theology!

We cannot get away from a thorough understanding of such basic notions of Christian life and action as redemption, salvation, liberation, new life, new man in Christ, kingdom of God, etc.

This gospel is announced as good news, a happy novelty, a marvelous offer, and soon we find

97

ourselves accumulating adjectives with growing meaning, until our words begin to falter, and we worship.

Such salvation is no human accomplishment. It is accomplished by God in Christ and is offered without discrimination to all mankind. This salvation, according to the New Testament, is a total liberation. It is to bring us from darkness into light, from loneliness to fellowship, from selfishness to love; it is liberation from oppression of every sort, including the most secular ones; it is freedom from sin and death. It is liberation from a course of life that leads unto death.

The church through the centuries has understood this as a personal reality. The work of Christ is interpreted as the redemption of the person in his or her whole being. Certainly this cardinal aspect is not to be obscured, but is to be considered as the specific task of the church. Yet we cannot restrict it to the individual realm, because it is simultaneously a social reality. The individual does not remain in loneliness; through love he enters at once into a community. He begins with the community of the church and comes to know the fact of fellowship, fraternal communion. But at the same time he knows himself to be called to give himself in love to the whole society that surrounds him. We cannot forget that Jesus preached the kingdom of God.

The realm of God is an absolute order in which the will of the Father is fulfilled. Wherever the will of God is done, there is the kingdom of God. This kingdom presupposes the redemption of man and society, and even of the whole creation, according to Romans 8, and moves toward that time when all things that are on earth and in heaven become one in God through Christ, as we read in Ephesians.

We enter this kingdom by responding to his call, and by gratefully accepting the generous offer from God. Once within the kingdom we are called to behave as citizens of it everywhere, including where the will of God is not obeyed. We cannot bring in the kingdom. We are called to be witnesses to its reality by living lives consecrated to the purposes of God and by giving ourselves in love and service to our neighbors.

This is a reality which includes the past, the present, and the future. It is something God has done once for all in Jesus Christ through all he was, said and did, in his life, in his death and in his resurrection. That is why a Christian, when asked the rather impertinent question of when was he saved, could answer: "In the first century when Christ died for me." But God is alive today and continues his work of salvation. Salvation for us can become a present reality. This is not a question of a historical past even a personal one, as when somebody refers to the date of his conversion, or new birth. It is not something we can write into a square of a calendar of years past. It is something of the here and now, which calls us every day to a decision. The Christian life is an ever-deciding-to-do what he commands.

At the same time it is a future reality, the consummation of that which lies not in the past or in the present, but which projects itself forward to a historical future here on earth. This element is present frequently in the New Testament. We are called upon to grow in the knowledge and grace of our Lord Jesus Christ. Here we come upon personal and social sanctification, the bringing of everything into subjection to Christ. But at the same time it transcends history and time and points to a salvation to be fulfilled and consummated beyond history, at a time when everything will be made new, including a new heaven and a new earth, when the kingdoms of this world become absorbed and transformed into the kingdom of God and his Christ, as we read in Revelation.

Now let us make a venture and try to answer the question. What does it mean to proclaim the gospel? What are the ways or modes of our proclamation? I will answer with several words.

The first is *message*. It is a question of communicating the message. It is a verbal affair. It has been said again and again that the word is in crisis. Words have lost their value through hypocrisy, lying, and trivialization. But words must be restored to their original worth because we cannot get rid of words. To speak is something peculiar to human beings. We could not cease to talk without being dehumanized. In a consultation on evangelism that we had in Bolivia some years ago, somebody tried to convince us that we ought to keep silent and give a mute witness. But in order to do this he employed a multitude of words. The documents produced on the subject were full of words, wise and not so wise words. In any case, this thing of silence with regard to evangelization has no biblical basis. The New Testament employs every Greek term there is to say that we have to speak the gospel, to witness to it with our lips. What is important is that all this talk be the gospel and not something else. It is important that we should say what God has told us, and not that we should be an echo of the words of the street. Sometimes, a proclamation is called "prophetic" when it really only echoes the theories in vogue, outside the church. "Let the church be the church" was a voice of order during the crisis of the Second World War. Maybe it should be repeated again today. "Faith comes from what is heard, and what is heard comes by the preaching of Christ." The Gospel is not something that can be guessed: it must be proclaimed to us; the secret must be openly told, for there is no other way of knowing it. Christ must be announced. Now this word must become flesh in us, so that it becomes the life of our life. The verbal message cannot be understood outside the context of a genuinely Christian life, put to the service of God and man in the interests of the kingdom. What makes our message intelligible is a life of love. Without it our words are but a sounding gong or a clanging cymbal.

The second word is *worship*. Surely worship is far more than a liturgical act. It is the opening of the whole person, in mind, feeling, and will to the truth, the love and power of God so that we may be imbued by his Spirit. This involves our whole life. But the worship service of the community gathered in his name is the expression of that total attitude in an act of praise, in response to the commandment: "Thou shall love thy God and him alone shall thou worship." To participate in the worship service of the church, if it is divorced from daily obedience, is to turn it into hypocrisy, and it ceases to be worship. What happens at the worship hour? Sadly enough many a time we must confess that nothing has happened. It is far worse if we become used to having nothing happen. Can we expect people to overcome growing obstacles in the road laid out by our modern life if the hour of worship is not significant?

Certainly there is a grave responsibility laid on the preacher and those who lead the worship service. But a serious responsibility also belongs to the congregation which, with its apathy, quenches the Spirit.

A worship service can never be boring if the Spirit is present. Something always happens. And if the worship service is related to the real problems of life, and if in it we share our faith, our hopes, and frustrations, our successes, and our failures, and as a brotherhood united in love we truly worship God, then the service of worship will be tremendously vital. If we need to change the forms of worship let us do so. Only let us remember that more than a question of forms, it is a question of attitudes. And this is something that has to do with every one of us, and not only with those who lead the worship service. Let us put ourselves at the disposal of the Spirit so he will enlighten our imagination and sanctify it so we may find the best ways to worship God significantly.

Then, we hear much about the *koinonia* groups. It is a Greek word which means fellowship, communion. These are groups in which we love each other enough to care about the problems of our brother or sister and do something about them. I don't believe it is a question of organizing the groups; they ought to be born, and grow by contagion. Nor need we institutionalize them permanently. I can imagine that a group of about ten should meet to pray and study and discuss together for a relatively short period and then dissolve, and then each member should gather around him another similar group, and so on. The important thing is that the Spirit be present. Fellowship is that reality of love exemplified in the inner life of the Christian community. Each Christian congregation should be so united in faith, hope, and love that it should give an example of what a society organized in harmony with the kingdom of God ought to be. Jesus prayed that we should love each other "so that the world may believe." Our fellowship has therefore a missionary intent. This is loaded with the most serious consequences, for the love of which the Bible speaks is not theoretical and sentimental, but practical and concrete. "But if a man has enough to live on, and yet when he sees his brother in need shuts up his heart against him, how can it be said that the divine love dwells in him? Love must not be a matter of words or talk; it must be genuine and show itself in action" says the First Epistle of John. What does it mean that in the church there are those who have much money and others who suffer hunger and need? How do we translate love there? Our congregational love may shine because of lack of love in the world, but it is far from being what God expects from us. There are enough examples of authentic love outside the church to fill us with shame.

Another word is *study*. In First Peter we read: "Gird up your minds." The idea is to be ready for tough work with your mind. Many people speak of a simple gospel. I don't care if it is simple, but I do care that it should be the gospel. In any case I don't want it more simple than the New Testament. Read the profound letters of the New Testament and you will find out that simplicity may be a mythological affair. Anselm said something to the effect that we don't begin by understanding but by believing; but once having believed, it would be sheer nonsense not to try to understand what we have believed. The New Testament also burdens us with the task of giving reason for the faith that is in us. What does all this mean but that we have the responsibility of studying? We need to study our faith and to study the world to which that faith is to be communicated. This is part of the strengthening of the congregation for its missionary task.

We then have to make our contribution to the life of the congregation. We cannot share our emptiness. We must take heed that our spirit shall not go empty: this is our part, or our duty towards the brethren. This requires discipline in our devotional life. We must at all costs find time for prayer and Bible study. Don't tell me we have no time when so much is wasted before TV sets, for example. And this is only one example among many.

Another word that expresses concern for the mission of the church is one that in my country has become very common: *Project the church into the community.* The church should not be turned inward upon itself and become ingrown but it should grow outward. Yes, but let us remember that the church should project itself in love and service and concern. It is the whole community and not only the pastor who must go out into the surrounding community. It is well and good that the pastor should lead but if he goes alone then the missionary orientation of the church is lost.

Jesus said of himself that he did not come to be served but to serve. He gave us examples again and again of faithful service. In his teachings as well he emphasized the importance of service, which to him was the sign of real greatness. It is through permanent service to others that our fellowship of love can go out to reach all persons. The Christian and the church are in the world to serve and not to be praised. The church needs to be present in the community and claim as her own its problems. They cannot be foreign to them. She must present these problems to God in intercessory prayer and in love give witness to her faith. Christian people must go into all works of goodness and justice. In each of those institutions that promote the good, be they secular or religious, our members ought to be represented by some of the fellowship. In every sphere of daily activity, Christian people are to be actively

103

involved so that the church may be a living presence even if it be unknown, and even if she does not go about broadcasting that she does it out of love. This service to the community must be given in the local situation and in the wider regional ones as well. Wherever there is a need, be it material, economic, moral, social, political, intellectual, emotional, physical, or spiritual, there is the mission of the church. There is God calling her to give herself in love and service.

The social reality in which we live in Latin America presents a painful picture. There are among us millions of people who are born poor, and poor they must die, because there is no other alternative for them. They are people who cannot develop in a normal way their bodies, their minds, or their souls. Millions will have to die soon in a time when the span of life has increased for other sections of our modern society. And this not because they are less able, less intelligent, or less willing, but because the economic structures under which they live do not allow them to become free from restricted possibilities. The rich become richer at the expense of the poor who thus become poorer. This is not only true of individuals or local communities; it is also true of entire nations. Remember that underdevelopment is not a previous step to development. Underdevelopment in some areas of the world is rather the consequence of overdevelopment in others. Now what does it mean to be Christian in such a situation? How can the church express its love for the oppressed? As a world Methodist community, how can we avoid cancelling out our witness by our participation in all this evil? If we side with the oppressor and not with the oppressed, do we not see that we cannot witness authentically to Christ, nor even make intelligible the witness of those who give themselves in sacrifice for the poor of the earth?

Let me say a word about *pastoral work*. We understand the pastoral task as belonging to the community as a whole and not exclusively to the ministers. I participated once in a Consultation on

Pastoral Work in the River Plate. There somebody said that pastoral work could be done today more efficiently by the psychiatrist than by the Christian minister or lay person. My answer is no! The pastoral function does not coincide with the psychiatric one, though it may have points of contact. The pastoral function is not mainly to bring peace and inward serenity. On the contrary, it must sometimes bring unrest to a too comfortable conscience. The pastoral function is to mediate Jesus Christ, and this is not done by technical knowledge (however useful such knowledge may be to avoid serious mishandling in pastoral care), but rather by a living and personal faith. There is an immense task to perform in our modern society. There are many whom we need to comfort in sorrow, to strengthen in struggle, to enlighten in perplexity. We need to awaken their conscience, to give them orientation on the road, and to help so many who have lost their way to come to know Christ who loves them and is always near them, even when they are not aware of him.

And now a final word on evangelism as part of our mission. There is need for a continuous evangelism. One of our pastors said to a committee: "There is no need for special efforts of evangelism, if something is happening in the life of the church. In such a case evangelism in fact would be taking place; and if nothing is happening then, evangelism cannot take place." There is tremendous truth in that. If the congregations are living communities of love and joy, they will be attracting people to Christ. And if not, they will be defeating whatever evangelistic efforts they may launch. In this, again, we must not stick to certain methods of evangelism as if they were sacred, forgetting that they do not appear in the New Testament at all. Therefore we must call into question every method and see whether it continues to fulfill today the purpose it served in the past. In any case, under the guidance of the Spirit we must venture into practicing evangelism in many different ways.

The proclamation of the message communicated by speech and deed, by worship and fellowship, by social and personal action and service, is an integral part of the total mission that is before us. May God help us to fulfill it in his spirit!

A Theology
for Evangelism

Theology no doubt is capable of various and sundry definitions, especially in times such as ours, when special groups in society have their own vocabulary, and words that used to have general usage are co-opted by them for their own private designations, often quite different from what the public at large understands a word to mean.

Gay in the English language is a typical example. In times past, most people would have characterized their parties and social events as gay, for they thought of the word as meaning lighthearted, carefree, full of fun, and given over to entertainment and pleasure; but now many might hesitate before accepting an invitation to a "gay" party, since the word has been taken over by organized homosexuals as the adjective designating their movement. The Gay Liberation Movement means something quite different from "merry." It is serious, dead serious, as we readily see from the demands it is making on society, and now even on the church herself.

Liberation, too, has a different connotation in many circles from what it used to have. The New Testament says that Jesus came to preach deliverence and to set the captives free. But when Russian invaded Czechoslovakia, she offered as an explanation the need to liberate the

Czechoslovakian people, though many of them, I am sure, would have preferred the "slavery" they had to the "liberation" they got.

One of the newest liberation movements of world-wide dimensions is the Women's Liberation Movement. I don't know how it is elsewhere, but in the United States the women already own and control a very large proportion of the capital wealth of the land. They are not proposing to be liberated from that. Naturally, they have duties in the home, responsibility for managing household affairs, and the rearing of children on a day-to-day basis, which men do not have. I presume many are advocating liberation from those chores. But, generally, what women's liberation stands for is less a deliverance from bondage than it is an empowerment for greater control over the affairs of society, a bigger share in the management of the world. They are tired of working behind the scenes. They do not want to work through their husbands and sons, but directly, in their own rights, receiving the credit themselves for the good that is accomplished.

If Susannah Wesley had lived in the twentieth century instead of the eighteenth century, and if she had joined the Women's Liberation Movement, she would have applied for the living at Epworth rather than her husband, and, in my opinion, she would have done a much better job of it than poor old Samuel ever did. I do have some reservations, I must confess, that she would ever have been as successful with the Revival as were her sons, John and Charles. In that instance, I am grateful that she was content to be a mother. It was through them that she had her share in the founding of The Methodist Church.

Not long ago I heard a theologian of some repute say that a theocentric concept of God is altogether outmoded and must be abandoned before we can advance in our theology. I was bewildered by what he said, for *theism* and *God* in religious parlance are almost synonyms, since the former is a derivation of the latter; for just to believe in God demands a theistic interpretation of the universe and everything that is in it.

We can, to be sure, offer an explanation of the world in which we live that does not require our belief in God; and there are, as you know, about as many theistic interpretations as there are theologians to make them. But once having accepted the notion of God, we are bound to consider everything else in relation to him, even if we say, as the Deists did, that he, perhaps, is not interested in his creation, and, having made it, leaves it to operate independently of him, according to the laws of its own inner being. But the notion of a non-theistic God is, so it appears to me, a self-contradiction, like the notion of a snake that is not a reptile, a bear that is not a mammal, and a man and a woman who are not human beings. The only way to have a non-theistic God is to re-define both theism and God in a way to make them mutually exclusive, and I am sure this is what the theologian must have done in order to have a talking point. Unfortunately for me, however, the reason he felt he had to do this never became apparent.

People nowadays seem more interested in God-talk than they are in God himself. It is as though we pattern and design God by our coversations about him rather than reflect on the things we say that we, through scripture, tradition, and experience, know God to be. This God-talk leaves the impression that our deity can be tailor-made, like a suit of clothes, to fit whatever interest, desire, or concern we may have at the time.

Theology, as a scientific discipline, antedates Christianity by more than a generation, and it comes to us by way of Rome rather than Jerusalem. What we have labeled 'natural theology' was first introduced into the vocabulary of thinking people by M. Terrentius Varro, a contemporary of the orator Cicero. He used the word to distinguish between an account of God that is strictly true and other accounts of him that are either poetic or pragmatic.

Homer, for example, was the best narrator in antiquity of poetic or mythical theology. The gods on

Mount Olympus are fascinating characters, and the stories about them are delightful, forming the contents of the best epochal poetry imaginable. Their object, however, is not truth but entertainment. As far back as the Periclean Age, enlightened people, such as Socrates and Plato, accepted these stories as no more than expressions of the imaginations of poets and artists.

Pragmatic theology, in contrast, had to do with the support of the state and its institutions. Those beliefs were concocted by statesmen and politicians to assure unity and the obedience of the people to the rulers who had been set over them. It had no more relationship to truth than did poetic theology. Yet it was more immediate in its practical utility, since society was apt to be orderly or disorderly, depending on how well the citizens accepted and practiced its tenets. If Romans believed Caesar to be a divine being, they were more apt to obey his edicts and to defend his person. Worship and service generally go hand in hand.

Varro advocated a different theology entirely. His was based on philosophy, which in that day was metaphysical, and sought a comprehensive view of the totality of things rather than a concentrated examination of only one of its many parts. What could be inferred about deity, from a careful and complete observation of nature, both organic and inorganic, was his purpose in theologizing. Thus his definition of theology was the scientific study of God in relationship to the universe he has made.

Now when we essay the task of delineating a theology for evangelism, we run the risk of concocting a pragmatic theology; that is, of constructing a set of beliefs that will promote the expansion of Christianity, the numerical increase of the institutional church, and the empowerment of organized religion, especially our particular brand of it, to become more influential and powerful and determinative in the affairs of the world. In other words, pragmatic theology is almost inevitably the intellectual justification for ecclesiastical triumphalism. When we say that the church's business is to save the world, it is so easy for us to mean, without actually realizing it, that it is the church's responsibility to make the world subservient to the church and altogether obedient to her commands. It is the tendency of the servant to identify himself with his master and to do his good works, not to glorify God, but to win for himself a reputation of honor and esteem.

The only way to escape this danger is to try to understand evangelism itself theologically, that is, to set it in the total Christian perspective, realizing that, as an activity or mission of the church, it must be defined doctrinally and therefore carried out in keeping with its nature as one among several of the important functions of our religion. In other words, we do not start out with evangelism, which is an activity, and seek to reason out a theological system by which to justify and to increase that activity. Our procedure should be the reverse of this. What is there about our theology that demands that we engage in evangelism? What is the doctrinal reason for our efforts to win other people to the Christian faith? Is there the conviction that we cannot be faithful ourselves unless we persuade others to embrace the faith which we so ardently profess?

Evangelism is outwardly oriented. It is an activity that is always focused on the welfare of those we attempt to evangelize, never on the evangelists themselves. We are not Boy Scouts, Girl Scouts, or Good Scouts, seeking so many merit points on the way to becoming Eagle Scouts as we chalk up numbers in our evangelistic campaigns. The purpose of evangelism is always to improve the lot of those who are being evangelized. Therefore, Christian evangelism has as its theological raison d'etre the doctrine of the incarnation. Outside the New Testament, Saint Irenaeus was perhaps the first theologian to give clear and convincing expression of this belief, and his statement of it has become classic: "God became man in order that man might become godlike." A better contemporary translation of its full meaning, would be: "God became human in order that human beings might become divine."

111

Evangelism, however, presupposes the fact that people are capable of being evangelized, and what we style a theology of evangelism provides not only a doctrine that gives us the concern to become evangelists, but also the belief that those about whom we are concerned can be responsive to our appeal.

When Saint Columba and Saint Columban went as missionaries to the barbarians in the early Middle Ages, they had more than the zeal of apostles for the welfare of the people to whom they preached. They believed the barbarians would understand and appreciate their message. Otherwise, there was no purpose in leaving their native lands on such a venture. Missional effort is futile if it is nothing more than the work of the missionary.

Effective evangelism in our times rests on the assumption that the people to whom the Christian gospel is addressed are equipped with moral discrimination; that is, that they know basically the difference between right and wrong. Otherwise, there is no connecting link between the word spoken and the word heard, between the proclamation of the gospel and the people to whom it is proclaimed.

I like drama. Nothing amuses me more than to watch a play performed on stage. Like many of you, I have gone at the beginning of each decade since World War II to Oberammergau to see the Passion Play, even though the language is German, which is not my native tongue. I have been told that one of the best ways to learn a new language is to go to the theater and to listen carefully to the dialogue as the action unfolds before one's eyes on the stage. A Chinese who spoke relatively good English told me that he learned all he knew by watching old American films. Some of you might question whether it was really English he learned, or not.

But this won't work by trying to listen to a lecture in a language about which one has no knowledge at all. What would happen to a Frenchman, religiously, if the only instruction he got was from sermons spoken in

Japanese? The loneliest day for me in my travels abroad is always Sunday, if I am in a land where the language spoken is one I do not understand. I go to church. I sit quietly in the congregation as songs are sung, prayers are prayed, and the sermon preached, but all I hear are noises, though I take for granted they are joyful noises made unto the Lord from one of his lands.

Evangelism presupposes rudimentary moral sensitivity on the part of everybody. It takes for granted that spiritual discernment is basic to human nature. "No man living," writes John Wesley, "is entirely destitute of what is vulgarly called natural conscience," which he further defines by saying, "Conscience then is that faculty, whereby we are at once conscious of our thoughts, words, actions, and of their merit or demerit, of their being good or bad, and, consequently, deserving either praise or censure. . . . Can it be denied that something of this is found in every man born into the world?"

Perhaps this, after all, is the enduring lesson of Pentecost. When the Spirit descended on the disciples in the upper room in Jerusalem, and they received tongues of fire, what the people outside heard from them, they heard in their own language, whatever it was; that is, there was something moral in their nature that made them responsive to the higher morality about which the disciples, especially Peter, were talking.

We are made in the image of God. This is not some special gift conferred only on Jews and Christians. The Old Testament claim by the Jews that they were God's chosen people did not exclude others from the benefits of creation or deny that God had breathed his divine breath of life on the parcel of dirt out of which they had been fashioned. Nor in the New Testament did the name which designated the followers of Jesus deprive others of their status as human beings. The apostle Paul admitted frankly, and reminded Christians never to forget, that God made of one blood all people to dwell on the face of the earth. The heathen were right in their assertion that we are all his offspring.

113

That means that the task of living as human beings is a universal task, and the obligation of attaining the highest status of humanity is one that we share with all others, regardless of their religious affiliation, or even of whether or not they profess any religious conviction at all. Basic intelligence and conscience are natural endowments. Both of the categories of Immanuel Kant, that of 'practical reason' as well as that of 'pure reason' are grounded in human nature unqualified by any outside resource not contained within itself. "Act," wrote Kant, "as if the maxim of thy action were to become a universal law of nature." And he felt that anyone, no matter who he is, is capable of such action, whether his religion be Confucian, Buddhist, Taoist, Shinto, Moslem, Jewish, or Christian. Though I realize this is anachronistic, it is reasonable to assume that Kant might expect this of a Marxist, that is, a disciple of atheistic materialism as well. There must be a scale of values, or at least the capability of understanding moral worth and evaluating human behavior, inherent in human nature itself.

This is why Christians can, and should, engage in dialogue with peoples of other faiths. This is different from ecumenical conversations. Ecumenical conversations are within the Christian family. They are among people who accept Jesus Christ as Lord and Savior. But conversations with others of a different religion carry us beyond the bounds of our own faith. Denominational differences are largely sociological in nature, and we date their origin to specific periods in history and cite the circumstances and conditions in which they arose. But religious differences are differences of revelation. Their ideational, or ideological, data are not the same. Hinduism, for example, has its objective escape from life and a complete break with the cycle of perpetual existence, whereas Islam and Christianity set as their goals the attainment of life eternal. The hope of the one is nonexistence, while that of the other is joy forever in heaven.

Nonetheless, the devotees of all religions, as well as

the people who deny the validity of any religion at all, are human beings with conscience and the obligation of living here and now as satisfying and creative a life as it is possible to live. In achieving this, people are capable of perceiving and practicing compassion, acts of mercy and kindness, charity, and all those virtues which have adorned non-Christian civilizations as well as our own. Justin Martyr, one of the first apologists in Christian history, included Homer and Socrates among the worthies of Christianity, on the basis of their moral and intellectual attainments; and our Lord himself said that he who is not against us is for us, for he recognized his sheep outside the Christian fold.

This recognition of the universality of the discernment of value and the appreciation of right and wrong among humankind rests on the theological doctrine of creation, the *imago Dei*, that we are all made in the image of God, and in our own Wesleyan tradition, on prevenient grace, which is indigenous to human nature itself. "In morality," wrote Bosanquet, "we know that the good purpose is real, in religion we believe that nothing else is real." And Immanuel Kant taught that there is nothing anywhere that is good without qualification, except good will. We perceive, know, and appreciate this, simply because we are human beings.

Conscience, or the recognition of value, is less an element, or aspect, of evangelism than it is a prolegomenon to evangelism. Though the *imago Dei* and prevenient grace are essential to any doctrine of creation which undergirds the evangelistic effort, that effort itself is initiated by other, more compelling, convictions of the Christian faith. The best set of lectures on evangelism that it was ever my privilege to hear on the Sam P. Jones Foundation at Emory University was given by the late W. E. Sangster of Central Hall, Westminster, London under the title "Let Me Commend My Saviour." The thesis he developed was far less an argument than it was a witness. It did not disparage other religions, or criticize irreligious ideologies and philosophies of life. Rather, assuming the human

115

disposition for comparison and assessment as well as the capacity to evaluate in terms of merit and ultimate worth, the lectures he gave set forth in direct fashion what Jesus Christ and the religion he founded had done for the speaker, and why he believed that it was essential to the total welfare of everybody else.

I worked on a small committee from the Council of Bishops in The United Methodist Church in the United States to formulate a message on evangelism. In preparation for our work, we wrote several responsible Methodists within the denomination for their suggestions. A professor at one of our seminaries, a person who, before the merger, had been a leader in the Evangelical United Brethren branch of our church, wrote that in our zeal for interreligious understanding and cooperation we should not feel compelled to appreciate the tenets of other religions to the extent that we disparage our own. It is our primary responsibility, he said, to give a reason for the faith that is within us and to encourage others to embrace that faith.

In the pluralism of these times, I am persuaded that our methods of evangelism must be far more conciliatory and open to the opinions, yea, *convictions* of people of other faiths and ideologies than ever before. We cannot go out, as did the servants of the king, in Jesus' parable, into the highways and hedges and compel people to come in. Our method is that of the "soft sell" rather than the "hard sell." In talking to them about the reasons for our commitment, we must be willing in exchange to hear the reasons for theirs. We can best trust that their natural apparatus of evaluation under the tutelage and inspiration of God's spirit will prompt them to accept Jesus Christ as Lord and Savior. What happens in such instances is not our responsibility. Our responsibility is to witness to what he has done for us. That witness is always more effective in example than it is in words. "Let your light so shine before men that they may see your good works, and glorify your Father in heaven."

Dom Gregory Dix, in perhaps as fine an essay as has

ever been written on the ministry in the early church, shows that the New Testament apostle had his prototype in the Jewish *shaliach* of the Old Testament. The *shaliach* was a friend, or maybe just a slave, sent as a plenipotentiary from an important personage to act for him in such a way that the action of the plenipotentiary was the action of the principal himself. What Jesus did on earth committed God in heaven to stand by and validate his actions. Likewise, the apostles were entrusted so completely with our Lord's mission after the ascension that in speaking for Christ it was as if Christ himself had spoken through them. Jesus said to Peter, "Whatsoever you bind on earth shall be bound in heaven, and whatsoever you loose on earth shall be loosed in heaven."

Likewise, whenever a Christian witnesses truly and sincerely to Christ, he has potentially, depending, of course, on the responsiveness of the hearer, the power and effectiveness of his divine Lord. That is why if a person is a genuinely committed Christian, he cannot restrain himself from being an evangelist. He firmly believes our Lord's promise, "And I, if I be lifted up from the earth, will draw all men unto myself."

Evangelism is always *anamnesis* and anticipation. It is a clear remembrance of what God has done and an unwavering faith that he will do it again. It both proclaims the mighty acts of God in history and promises their fulfillment for good in the lives of those who believe. Pope Gregory the Great said simply of Jesus, whom he offered as the Savior of all who would accept him, "while cleansing us with the water of salvation, He did not screen his face from the spitting of perfidious men, . . . while saving us from being poisoned from our sins, He did not shrink from offering His head to thorns; that He took bitter gall in His thirst in order to inebriate us with everlasting sweetness, . . . and that He was the life passed to death that He might prepare life for those who were dead." The doctrine of salvation, with its twin foci of atonement and reconciliation, is the theological explanation of the impetus to, or initial drive in,

117

evangelism. It is the doctrinal heart of the Christian faith.

As the heart keeps the body alive, so our belief in salvation by the grace of God through faith in Jesus Christ keeps us constantly employed in the evangelistic enterprise, offering to others, in God's name, what he has given and continues always to give us. But what, practically speaking, is this? What really happens when people are truly evangelized? What, precisely, are the results we can expect from the enterprise? Those questions, of course, in compliance with our theme, are all inferential. Both the posing of them and the answers they yield are determined by our theology.

A Moslem, for example, would not ask them; indeed, they would not occur to him, since his religion is largely dictated by fate, so that the future of the individual, of his society, of his nation, and of the world, is in the hands of Allah, who does in each and every instance what he wills. Historically speaking, there has been displayed in Islam a form of evangelism in which the individual escaped slavery through a change in his religious affiliation, but the isolation of Mecca and Medina to all except the disciples of Mohammed stands as the symbol of exclusiveness and the "closed shop" attitude of that religion to the outside world. Hinduism, being largely eclectic, is more receptive than aggressive; while Buddhism, Confucianism, and Taoism are anthropological rather than theological, making salvation a human burden rather than a divine gift. Marxist Communism, which has come to be a religion, and must be reckoned as such, is economic and political in motivation. It makes its appeal to classes, societies, and nations, with a definite plan for their reconstitution, rather than to individuals, in terms of personal needs and aspirations. Even Judaism, out of which Christianity arose and from whose prophets much of the grandeur of its morality derives, is still racially based, as exemplified by the nation of Israel and by Jewish communities with the same beliefs, habits, and policies, wherever they are in the world. By thinking of God always as the God of

118

Abraham, Isaac, and Jacob, the Jews have maintained their racial integrity and have preserved themselves as Jews regardless of where they have lived throughout all history.

Christianity, in a unique way, has been expansive by nature and universal in scope, advancing beyond national lines, penetrating into all classes and castes of society, and disregarding race; for the object of its concern has never been just the places where people live, but the individual persons who live there, each and every one, in terms of his needs and what he ought to have as a child of God. It was not for the Jewish nation, the Greek city-state, or the Roman Empire, that Jesus died. It was for Peter, James, and John; for Luke, and for the centurion Cornelius. Jesus did not come into the world either to promote communism or to preserve capitalism. His gospel is not addressed exclusively either to the Labor Party or to the Tories, though it is offered just as freely to Ted Heath as to Harold Wilson, and can use Raymond George as well as Lord Soper for its proclamation.

What happens through evangelism? People are transformed. Their orientation is changed. Life no longer revolves around themselves and their self-interests, but they become creative and constructive partners in a wholesome, compassionate, and mutually supportive community, which finds its center in the church, which expands to influence, change, and even to embrace and include secular society, and which reaches its fulfillment outside time, in the everlasting kingdom of God.

No matter how unselfish we are in philanthropy, no matter how great our zeal in changing the structures of society, no matter how hard our work for justice and equal opportunity for all, we will never have a good social order and a good world until there are good people to inhabit it, people who individually, one by one, are transformed by the grace of God into new creatures, who in their character and behavior display the virtues of Jesus Christ. This is the purpose of evangelism. Theologically we believe in the doctrine of

119

sanctification, moral and spiritual perfectibility in this life. And our evangelistic effort is to bring this about everywhere. As Christians, we cannot afford to attempt less in the name of Jesus. And should we succeed by his grace, what is there really more to do? To be completely human is really to live unselfishly for others, as Jesus Christ lived and died unselfishly for us.